THE ULTIMATE

KRAFT

PHILADELPHIA

COOKBOOK

EBURY
PRESS

NOTES ON RECIPES:

Where Philadelphia is stated in the ingredients list it refers to full-fat Philadelphia.
Where Philadelphia Chives or Philadelphia Garlic & Herbs is stated in the ingredients
list it refers to Philadelphia Light Chives or Philadelphia Light Garlic & Herbs.
Recipes have only been tested with the type of Philadelphia stated in the ingredients
list, unless otherwise specified.

All spoon measures are level unless otherwise specified.
All eggs are medium unless otherwise specified.
All milk is semi-skimmed unless otherwise specified.
All fresh herbs, fruit and vegetables should be washed before use.
All eggs, pork and poultry should be thoroughly cooked.
Oven temperatures are for non fan-assisted ovens so should be adjusted accordingly.

The nutrition information refers to the main ingredients listed, not for seasoning to taste,
optional ingredients or serving suggestions.
Equivalent as salt has been calculated from the sodium nutrition value for each recipe.

1 3 5 7 9 10 8 6 4 2

Published in 2010 by Ebury Press, an imprint of Ebury Publishing
Ebury Publishing is a division of the Random House Group

Text © Kraft Foods 2010
Photography © All photographs © Ebury Press 2008 except: pages 2, 17, 31, 39, 40,
45, 51, 57, 58, 67, 69, 72, 75, 87, 89, 98, 110, 115, 129, 131, 135, 140, 159, 162, 169, 171,
174, 177, 183, 187, 189, 193, 195, 203, 219, 225, 228, 239, 240, 246, 265 © Dan Jones
Photography on pages 62, 65, 83, 137, 231, 261, 263, 268, 272, 283 © Kraft Foods
Australia 2002

The Random House Group Limited Reg. No. 954009

Addresses for companies within the Random House Group can be found at
www.randomhouse.co.uk

A CIP catalogue record for this book is available from the British Library

The Random House Group makes every effort to ensure that the papers used in our books
are made from trees that have been legally sourced from well-managed and credibly
certified forests. Our paper procurement policy can be found on www.randomhouse.co.uk

Design: Smith & Gilmour, London
Photography & styling: Will Heap, Adrian Lander, Rachel Jukes, Dan Jones
Food styling: Sarah Tildesley, Linda Brushfield, Sonja Edridge, Sal Henley.
Prop stylist: Morag Farquhra
Recipe research, development & testing: Emma Warner, Valerie Hemming & Wendy Strang
Editor: Helena Caldon
Printed and bound in China by C and C Offset Printing Co. Ltd
ISBN: 9780091939151

To buy books by your favourite authors and register for offers visit www.rbooks.co.uk
For more Philly recipes and ideas visit www.philadelphia.co.uk

contents

introduction

Welcome to *The Ultimate Philadelphia Cookbook*. Discover the cool, creamy taste of Philadelphia and why it is so much more than just a cream cheese. It's the ultimate ingredient that is the perfect partner for foods of every description – whether sweet or savoury, low-fat or luxurious, spicy or creamy.

If you love Philadelphia and would like a little inspiration on how to get the best out of this delicious cream cheese, this book is for you. Packed with over 170 recipes for soups, light meals, party bites and dips, fish, chicken, meat, pasta and risotto, vegetables and sweet treats, you'll be spoilt for choice for new ways to use your Philly.

In these pages we've gone beyond bagels spread with Philadelphia and topped with various delicious ingredients, or even the classic fruity cheesecakes (although we've included those too!) and we've given the Philly twist to a huge range of dishes including Spicy Bean and Tomato Soup, Tuna and Olive Ciabatta, Salmon and Creamy Lentils, Chicken and Leek Pie, Sirloin Steak, Creamy Mushroom Risotto and Marbled Warm Chocolate Fudge Cake. Read on and you'll discover that armed with a tub of Philadelphia, the possibilities are endless …

From its humble beginnings in New York in 1872 at the hands of American dairyman William Lawrence, this cream cheese became known as Philadelphia in 1880 (inspired by the city that was then considered the home of top-quality food). Phenix Cheese Company bought the trademark in 1903, but it was a merger with Kraft foods in 1928 that took Philadelphia cream cheese further afield, reaching the UK in 1960. Now, after nearly 150 years, Philadelphia is sold in over 80 countries worldwide and has earned its place in myriad cuisines and cooking styles.

Whether the dishes are simple or elaborate, are intended as snacks or for entertaining, one thing they all have in common is that the methods are straightforward and clearly explained in simple steps.

All the recipes in this book have been tried and tested in our Philadelphia kitchen and, most importantly, tasted by a team of enthusiasts, until we have achieved perfect results and mouthwatering combinations. To help you get the most out of these dishes, we've also added some helpful cooking tips to the recipes along the way.

Each recipe also states how much preparation and cooking time is required to make each dish, so you can pick and choose according to how much time you have available. And if you're watching your weight, the nutritional breakdowns for each recipe allow you to have a little (or a lot!) of what you fancy.

We hope you'll be inspired by this ultimate collection of delicious recipes – enjoy!

spicy parsnip soup / creamy broccoli soup / leek and potato soup / pumpkin soup / spicy bean and tomato soup / pea soup / broad bean, chive philly and ham soup / scallop soup / seafood chowder / chicken and mushroom soup / creamy bean soup

SOUPS

spicy parsnip soup

serves 4–5 / prep time 10 minutes / cook time 35 minutes

2 tbsp olive oil
2 onions, chopped
1kg parsnips, peeled and
    diced into 3cm cubes
1 tbsp curry paste
1½ litres hot vegetable stock
100g Philadelphia Light
fresh chopped flatleaf parsley,
    to garnish

HEAT the oil in a large saucepan, add the onions and cook over a moderate to high heat for 1–2 minutes until softened. Add the parsnips and cook, covered, over a low heat for 5 minutes with the lid on, to sweat the vegetables.

STIR in the curry paste and cook for a minute, then add the hot stock. Cover and simmer for 20–25 minutes until the parsnips are soft.

ADD three-quarters of the Philly to the soup and blend with a hand blender or in a liquidiser until smooth. Season to taste. Serve with the remaining Philly stirred into the soup and garnish with the parsley.

tip Sweating the vegetables means to cook them slowly in a covered pan until the juices start to run. This way of gently cooking vegetables adds more flavour to the soup.

Per serving: energy 243kcal, protein 6.8g, carbohydrate 31.4g, fat 10.9g, equivalent as salt 2.2g

creamy broccoli soup

serves 4 / prep time 10 minutes / cook time 40 minutes

1 tsp olive oil
1 onion, finely chopped
1 large potato, peeled and
    cubed (approx. 2cm)
1 head broccoli (approx. 300g),
    cut into pieces (including
    the stalk)
450ml vegetable stock
500ml hot water
100g Philadelphia Extra Light
1 tbsp skimmed milk
1 tsp freshly grated nutmeg

HEAT the oil in a large saucepan and gently fry the onion until softened. Add the potato, broccoli stalk, stock and hot water. Bring to the boil and simmer for 10 minutes.

ADD the broccoli florets and some seasoning and continue to simmer for about 15 minutes until all the vegetables are cooked. Take off the heat and purée with a hand blender or liquidiser until smooth.

ADD 75g of the Philly and place back over the heat until the Philly has melted. In a bowl, stir the milk into the remaining Philly and serve swirled onto the soup with a dusting of nutmeg.

tip Try serving this on a cold winter's day with crusty bread.

Per serving: energy 141kcal, protein 8.4g, carbohydrate 16.3g, fat 5.4g, equivalent as salt 1.0g

leek and potato soup

serves 4 / prep time 15 minutes / cook time 25 minutes

3 leeks (approx. 450g)
2 tsp olive oil
1 onion, finely chopped
1 litre vegetable stock
450g potatoes, diced
120g Philadelphia Light

CUT off one-third of a leek, slice it into very thin strips, then wash and blanch them in boiling water for 1 minute. Set aside. Cut the remaining leeks into slices and wash well.

HEAT the oil and gently cook the raw leeks and onion for 3 minutes to soften, add the stock and potatoes and cook with the lid on for 20 minutes until the vegetables are tender. Add the Philly and, using a hand blender or liquidiser, blend until smooth. Adjust the seasoning and serve garnished with the blanched strips of leek.

Per serving: energy 190kcal, protein 7.5g, carbohydrate 27.2g, fat 6.3g, equivalent as salt 2.0g

pumpkin soup

serves 6 / prep time 10–15 minutes / cook time 25 minutes

15g butter
1 onion, finely chopped
1 garlic clove, finely chopped
750g pumpkin, peeled, deseeded
    and diced into 3cm cubes
1 carrot, diced into 2cm cubes
450ml vegetable stock
450ml hot water
1 tbsp white wine vinegar
1 tsp ground cinnamon
½ tsp freshly grated nutmeg
2 tbsp Philadelphia Light
2 tbsp warm milk
chopped fresh sage, to garnish

MELT the butter in a large saucepan. Cook the onion and garlic over a gentle heat until the onion softens. Add the pumpkin, carrot, stock and hot water, then bring to the boil.

SIMMER for 15 minutes or until the vegetables are tender. Add the vinegar and spices and season to taste with black pepper.

TRANSFER the soup to a food processor and blend until smooth. Return to the pan. In a bowl, mix the Philly with the warm milk and swirl into the soup. Serve straight away with warm crusty bread.

tip Butternut squash can be used in this recipe instead of pumpkin. Both are perfect garnished with freshly chopped sage.

Per serving: energy 78kcal, protein 2.9g, carbohydrate 7.6g, fat 4.3g, equivalent as salt 0.7g

spicy bean and tomato soup

serves 4 / prep time 10 minutes / cook time 15 minutes

2 tsp olive oil
1 onion, finely chopped
1 tbsp curry paste (medium or hot,
    depending on your preference)
700g jar tomato passata
400g can chopped tomatoes
150ml vegetable stock
400g can black eye beans, drained
100g Philadelphia Light

HEAT the oil in a large saucepan, add the onion and cook for 1 minute. Add the curry paste and cook for a further minute.

ADD the passata, chopped tomatoes, stock and beans and simmer for 10 minutes with the lid on. Season to taste and serve with the Philly stirred in.

Per serving: energy 254kcal, protein 15.1g, carbohydrate 35g, fat 6.1g, equivalent as salt 1.8g

pea soup

serves 4 / prep time 10 minutes / cook time 10 minutes

2 tsp olive oil
1 small onion, finely chopped
1 garlic clove, crushed
450g frozen peas
550ml hot vegetable or chicken stock
120g Philadelphia Light

HEAT the oil in a medium-sized saucepan and gently fry the onion and garlic for 1 minute until softened. Add the peas with the stock and simmer for 5 minutes.

ADD 100g of the Philly and some black pepper and remove from the heat. Purée using a hand blender or a liquidiser until fairly smooth.

SERVE hot with the remaining Philly spooned on top, or alternatively chill and serve as a cold soup.

tip Try adding 1 tablespoon chopped fresh mint before blending and use fresh peas when in season.

Per serving: energy 150kcal, protein 9.3g, carbohydrate 13.7g, fat 6.6g, equivalent as salt 1.8g

broad bean, chive philly and ham soup

serves 4 / prep time 5 minutes / cook time 20 minutes

2 tsp olive oil
1 onion, chopped
1 celery stick, finely diced
1 litre vegetable stock
350g shelled broad beans (use fresh or frozen)
4 slices smoked ham, diced
120g Philadelphia Chives

HEAT the oil in a large saucepan and gently fry the onion and celery until soft but not browned.

POUR in the stock, add the beans and ham and simmer for 15 minutes until the beans are cooked.

WITH a slotted spoon, take out 3 spoons of beans and ham and set aside. Remove the soup from the heat, add in the Philly and blitz with a hand blender or liquidiser until smooth. Return the beans and ham to the pan, season to taste and heat through briefly.

Per serving: energy 162kcal, protein 13.1g, carbohydrate 10.9g, fat 7.5g, equivalent as salt 1.7g

scallop soup

serves 4 / prep time 25 minutes / cook time 25 minutes

1 carrot, peeled
1 leek, trimmed and washed
2 tsp olive oil
1 onion, finely chopped
550ml fish stock
150ml white wine
120g Philadelphia Light
2 tsp cornflour, mixed with
    2 tsp water
12 scallops

CUT the carrot and leek into very thin long strips (julienne). Blanch in boiling water for 2 minutes and then cool under cold water. Leave on one side.

HEAT the oil in a saucepan and gently cook the onion for 2 minutes to soften. Add the stock and wine and simmer with the lid on for 10 minutes. Add the Philly, stir until melted, then strain into a clean pan through a fine sieve.

ADD the cornflour and cook until the soup has thickened very slightly. Add the scallops and cook for 3–4 minutes, then add the vegetable strips, heat through for 1 minute and serve.

tip If you want a little more colour in the dish, griddle the scallops for 1–2 minutes on each side before adding to the soup.

Per serving: energy 161kcal, protein 8.5g, carbohydrate 13.3g, fat 5.9g, equivalent as salt 1.8g

seafood chowder

serves 6–8 / prep time 20 minutes / cook time 20–25 minutes

2 medium potatoes, peeled
   and cubed
1 tsp olive oil
1 leek, finely sliced
1 garlic clove, crushed
200g white fish (e.g. 2 small
   haddock fillets), skinned
198g can sweetcorn kernels,
   drained
180g Philadelphia Extra Light,
   softened
275ml skimmed milk
2 tbsp roughly chopped fresh
   flatleaf parsley, plus extra
   to garnish (optional)
100g peeled, cooked prawns

PLACE the potatoes in a large saucepan, cover with cold water and bring to the boil over a medium heat. When boiling, reduce the heat and simmer for 10 minutes or until the potatoes are tender.

HEAT the oil in a non-stick pan, and sweat the leek and garlic in the oil with the white fish placed on top, to steam, for about 5 minutes. When the fish is cooked, it should flake easily.

DRAIN the potatoes and add to the pan with the leeks, fish and remaining ingredients. Cook over a medium heat for 5–8 minutes, stirring occasionally, until the Philly has melted, all the ingredients have heated through and the chowder has thickened. Garnish with a little chopped parsley, if liked.

tip If you prefer a thinner chowder, simply add a little extra milk until the desired consistency is reached.

Per serving: energy 132kcal, protein 15.1g, carbohydrate 13.1g, fat 2.5g, equivalent as salt 1.2g

chicken and mushroom soup

serves 6 / prep time 10 minutes / cook time 25 minutes

1 tsp olive oil
1 leek, finely sliced
250g closed cup mushrooms, sliced
2 garlic cloves, finely chopped
600ml chicken stock
200g boneless, skinless chicken
    breast, thinly sliced
120g Philadelphia Light
fresh chives, finely chopped,
    to garnish

HEAT the oil in a large saucepan over a medium heat. Add the leek, mushrooms and garlic. Cook for 5–6 minutes or until tender.

ADD the stock and bring to the boil. Reduce the heat, add the chicken and simmer for another 5 minutes until the chicken is cooked through.

COMBINE the Philly with a little of the soup liquid in a bowl and mix until smooth. Stir the Philly mixture into the soup, season with black pepper and heat through gently. Garnish with chopped chives and serve with fresh crusty bread.

tip Once the Philly is added, make sure the soup is heated through gently and not boiled, or it may separate.

Per serving: energy 135kcal, protein 17.7g, carbohydrate 2.7g, fat 5.9g, equivalent as salt 1.0g

creamy bean soup

serves 6 / prep time 10 minutes / cook time 30–35 minutes

15g butter or margarine
1 red onion, thinly sliced
2 garlic cloves, crushed
600ml vegetable stock
2 medium potatoes, peeled
    and cut into small pieces
420g can mixed beans, drained
200ml milk
100g Philadelphia Light, softened
fresh flatleaf parsley, roughly
    chopped, to garnish

MELT the butter or margarine in a large saucepan, add the onion and garlic and gently fry for about 5 minutes or until softened.

ADD the stock and potatoes, bring to the boil and cook for 10 minutes or until the potatoes are tender. Stir in the beans and simmer for a further 5 minutes.

STIR the milk into the Philly and then add to the soup. Continue to heat the soup gently for a few minutes until the Philly has completely melted. Serve in warmed bowls sprinkled with the fresh parsley.

tip For a smooth soup, blend in a food processor or liquidiser before adding the Philly. Return to the pan and continue as above.

Per serving: energy 174kcal, protein 9.1g, carbohydrate 19.9g, fat 7.0g, equivalent as salt 1.6g

baked sweet potatoes / philly tartiflette / colcannon / stuffed courgettes / garlic and herb baked mushrooms / chicken, chive and red pepper frittata / parma ham with asparagus and philly lemon sauce / philly and salmon quiche / cherry tomato and pancetta tart / smoked salmon scrambled eggs / red onion and rosemary savoury ramekins / breakfast muffins / chicken quesadillas / roast vegetable ciabatta / roast pumpkin bruschetta / smoked salmon bruschetta / tuna and olive ciabatta / chicken tikka bagels / prawn and rocket bagels / soufflé ramekins / sizzling chicken tortillas / classic smoked salmon bagels / tuna pittas / creamy hummous wrap / savoury bread cases / chicken salad wrap / philly steakwich / philly pan bagnat

LIGHT
MEALS

baked sweet potatoes

serves 2 / prep time 10 minutes / cook time 25 minutes (45 minutes in the oven)

2 medium sweet potatoes, washed
50g Philadelphia Light, softened,
    plus extra to serve
2 rashers back bacon, grilled and
    chopped
4 cherry tomatoes, quartered
salad leaves and snipped chives,
    to garnish

PREHEAT the oven to 200°C, gas 6. Prick the potatoes with a fork and microwave on High for 5 minutes. Transfer the potatoes to the oven for 20 minutes until cooked through. Alternatively, if you do not have a microwave, bake the potatoes in the oven for around 45 minutes until cooked through.

CUT the potatoes in half lengthways and scoop out the flesh with a spoon, keeping the skin intact, and mash with the Philly. Stir in the bacon and tomatoes and season with black pepper. Return the mash to the potato shells.

HEAT the grill to Medium. Place the potatoes under the grill until browned on top. Serve warm with a few dollops of Philly and some chives scattered over, and some salad leaves on the side.

tip Alternatively, mash the Philly straight into your cooked potato and top with the bacon and tomatoes.

Per serving: energy 195kcal, protein 9.6g, carbohydrate 20.9g, fat 8.5g, equivalent as salt 1.0g

philly tartiflette

serves 6 / prep time 10 minutes / cook time 45 minutes

1 tbsp olive oil
200g lean rindless bacon,
    chopped into pieces
1 onion, sliced
180g Philadelphia Garlic
    & Herbs
100ml single cream
400ml milk
½ x 15g pack fresh thyme,
    leaves removed
600g waxy potatoes cut into
    slices about the thickness
    of a pound coin
fresh green salad, to serve

PREHEAT the oven to 180°C/gas 4. In a frying pan, heat three-quarters of the oil and cook the bacon and onion.

MIX together the Philly, cream and milk so there are no lumps and add the thyme leaves. Pour into a saucepan and heat gently until not quite boiling.

WIPE over a 1-litre ovenproof dish with the remaining oil then scatter one-third of the onion and bacon into it. Arrange half of the potato slices on top, scatter with half the remaining bacon and onion and pour in half of the Philly mixture. Arrange the rest of the potatoes in the dish with the bacon and onions, pour over the rest of the Philly and bake in the oven for 45 minutes until the top is golden and the potatoes are cooked through. Serve with a green salad.

Per serving: energy 264kcal, protein 13.7g, carbohydrate 24.0g, fat 13.3g, equivalent as salt 1.5g

colcannon

serves 6 / prep time 10 minutes / cook time 15 minutes

450g new potatoes, washed
   and halved
450g Savoy cabbage, finely
   shredded
180g Philadelphia
1 tbsp wholegrain mustard
2 rashers streaky bacon

BOIL the potatoes in a saucepan of salted water until tender. Cook the cabbage in another pan with a tight-fitting lid and 1 tablespoon water until just wilted. Reduce the heat and remove the pan lid to dry off any moisture.

DRAIN the potatoes, crush with a fork and add to the cabbage with the Philly and mustard. Mix well to coat.

GRILL or dry-fry the bacon until really crispy and crumble over the top of the colcannon before serving.

tip Use mashed floury potatoes instead of new potatoes for a year-round dish.

Per serving: energy 191kcal, protein 6.5g, carbohydrate 15.1g, fat 12g, equivalent as salt 0.5g

stuffed courgettes

serves 4 / prep time 10 minutes / cook time 10 minutes

4 medium courgettes, halved
    lengthways
100g Philadelphia
198g can sweetcorn kernels,
    drained
40g cooked ham, diced
salad leaves, to garnish

USING a teaspoon, scoop out the seeds from the courgettes to form a boat shape. Cook them in a large saucepan of boiling water for 1–2 minutes until softened, then drain and place onto a grill pan.

MIX the Philly with the sweetcorn and ham and season with black pepper. Grill under a medium–hot grill for 3–4 minutes until starting to brown. Serve with a salad garnish.

tip This is a great way to use courgettes all year round, but particularly when they are less expensive in the summer months.

Per serving: energy 116kcal, protein 6.7g, carbohydrate 2.7g, fat 8.7g, equivalent as salt 1.8g

garlic and herb baked mushrooms

serves 4 / prep time 5–10 minutes / cook time 15–20 minutes

4 large open field mushrooms
3–4 tsp dry white wine
100g Philadelphia Garlic & Herbs
few sprigs of fresh thyme

PREHEAT the oven to 200°C, gas 6. Wipe the mushrooms with kitchen paper and remove the stalks.

STIR the white wine into the Philly and spread evenly over the cap of the mushrooms. Top each one with thyme sprigs and some black pepper.

WRAP each mushroom in a square of greaseproof paper, folding the paper over at the edges to form a seal, place onto a baking sheet and bake for 15–20 minutes. Serve in the paper or remove the paper and serve immediately.

tip If fresh thyme is unavailable, use a little dried thyme or fresh parsley sprigs instead. Lemon juice could be used instead of the wine.

Per serving: energy 62kcal, protein 3.6g, carbohydrate 1.2g, fat 4.4g, equivalent as salt 0.2g

chicken, chive and red pepper frittata

serves 2 / prep time 5–10 minutes / cook time 10 minutes

2 tsp olive oil
6–7 small new potatoes, cooked
   and diced
2 spring onions, chopped
½ red pepper, diced
1–2 tbsp fresh or frozen peas
½ chicken breast, cooked and diced
3 eggs, lightly beaten
60g Philadelphia Chives

PREHEAT the grill to Medium. Heat the oil in a small frying pan. Toss in the potatoes, vegetables and chicken. Fry on a medium heat for 3–4 minutes until warmed through.

REDUCE the heat to low. Add the eggs to the other ingredients and cook for a few minutes until the base is set and lightly browned.

DOT the Philly across the top of the frittata and pop under the grill until golden brown.

tip This is a great simple recipe for using up leftovers from the fridge. Try experimenting with different ingredients such as mushrooms, ham or fresh herbs for your favourite combination.

Per serving: energy 390kcal, protein 27.6g, carbohydrate 29.6g, fat 18.8g, equivalent as salt 0.8g

parma ham with asparagus and philly lemon sauce

serves 2 / prep time 5–10 minutes / cook time 8–10 minutes

100g Philadelphia Light
2–3 tbsp milk
juice of ½ lemon
200g fine asparagus
2 thick slices of crusty
    wholemeal bread
85g Parma ham

MIX together the Philly, milk and lemon juice in a small saucepan. Heat gently, stirring frequently until the Philly has melted; do not boil. Season with black pepper to taste.

STEAM the asparagus until tender but still firm.

PREHEAT the grill to Medium. Lightly toast the bread and grill the Parma ham until crispy. Place the toast on 2 serving plates, top with the asparagus and ham and serve with the warm sauce.

tip The lemon sauce is also lovely with griddled or barbecued chicken.

Per serving: energy 321kcal, protein 23.2g, carbohydrate 23.3g, fat 15.5g, equivalent as salt 2.7g

philly and salmon quiche

serves 4 / prep time 10 minutes / cook time 30 minutes

150g waxy potatoes, cooked
    and sliced
1 ready-made savoury shortcrust
    pastry case
170g fillet of salmon, cooked
    and flaked
3 eggs
120ml low-fat crème fraîche
120g Philadelphia Chives
3 sprigs of fresh dill, chopped

PREHEAT the oven to 180°C, gas 4. Lay the potatoes in the pastry case and scatter over the salmon pieces.

IN a bowl, mix together the eggs, crème fraîche, Philly and dill. Pour the mixture over the potatoes and salmon and bake for 30 minutes until golden and cooked through.

Per serving: energy 836kcal, protein 25.7g, carbohydrate 65.9g, fat 53.8g, equivalent as salt 1.5g

cherry tomato and pancetta tart

serves 9 / prep time 10 minutes / cook time 25–30 minutes

375g pack ready-rolled puff pastry
120g Philadelphia Extra Light
4 tbsp pesto
1 punnet cherry tomatoes, cut in half
4 slices pancetta, torn into pieces
handful of rocket

PREHEAT the oven to 200˚C, gas 6. Lay out the pastry on a baking sheet and score a line 3cm from the edge to create a border. Prick with a fork inside the border, then bake for 10 minutes until the pastry is puffed up and golden.

WHILE the pastry is cooking, mix 1 tablespoon Philly with the pesto and set aside.

AFTER 10 minutes, remove the pastry from the oven and press down the centre. Spread the remaining Philly over the centre area then top with the tomatoes and scatter over the pancetta. Season to taste.

COOK for 15–20 minutes until the tomatoes are cooked, scatter over a few rocket leaves and drizzle over the pesto and Philly mix to serve.

Per serving: energy 272kcal, protein 8.5g, carbohydrate 17.1g, fat 19.8g, equivalent as salt 1.0g

smoked salmon scrambled eggs

serves 4 / prep time 5 minutes / cook time 10 minutes

knob of butter
2 tbsp milk
6 large eggs, lightly beaten
100g Philadelphia Chives
4 thick slices of granary bread,
    toasted
100g smoked salmon, sliced

MELT the butter on a low heat in a non-stick saucepan. Beat the milk into the eggs, season with black pepper and pour into the pan. Cook very gently, stirring occasionally.

ADD spoonfuls of the Philly halfway through cooking and continue to stir occasionally until the eggs are cooked.

SERVE the creamy scrambled eggs with the hot toast and slices of smoked salmon.

tip Smoked salmon trimmings make this dish more economical and are perfect for stirring into the eggs just before the end of cooking.

Per serving: energy 344kcal, protein 25.5g, carbohydrate 22.3g, fat 17.6g, equivalent as salt 2.5g

red onion and rosemary savoury ramekins

serves 8 / prep time 20 minutes / cook time 20 minutes

1 tsp olive oil, plus extra for greasing
2 small red onions, peeled and finely
    chopped
1 tbsp fresh rosemary, finely
    chopped
200g Philadelphia Light
2 eggs, separated, plus 1 egg white
20g plain flour

PREHEAT the oven to 190˚C, gas 5. Heat the oil in a non-stick frying pan. Add the onions and rosemary and cook over a medium heat until the onions are soft but not coloured.

BEAT the Philly, egg yolks and flour together with an electric whisk, then stir in the onion and rosemary mixture. Whisk the 3 egg whites in a separate bowl until stiff peaks form then gently fold them through the cheese mixture. Season to taste.

DIVIDE the mixture between 8 individual greased ramekin dishes. Place on a baking sheet and bake for 18–20 minutes until golden. Serve immediately.

tip These ramekins make an excellent starter or light lunch served with a Greek salad.

Per serving: energy 79kcal, protein 4.6g, carbohydrate 4.2g, fat 4.9g, equivalent as salt 0.3g

breakfast muffins

serves 4 / prep time 10 minutes / cook time 15 minutes

4 rashers back bacon,
   rind removed
2 tsp white vinegar
4 English muffins, cut in half
   horizontally
2 medium tomatoes, sliced
100g Philadelphia
4 large eggs

HEAT the grill to Medium and cook the bacon until golden and crisp. Keep warm. Fill a medium–large pan three-quarters full with water and add the vinegar. Bring to the boil then reduce the heat to a simmer.

TOAST the muffins on both sides under the grill and grill the tomatoes on a piece of tin foil at the same time. Spread one half of each muffin with Philly and top the other halves with tomato slices.

POACH the eggs in the pan of simmering water for 2–3 minutes until just cooked. Place 2 muffin halves onto each plate, serving the poached eggs on the Philly half. Lay the bacon over the top of the other halves and serve.

Per serving: energy 432kcal, protein 24.4g, carbohydrate 44.9g, fat 18.3g, equivalent as salt 2.3g

chicken quesadillas

serves 2 / prep time 10 minutes / cook time 5 minutes

1 large cooked chicken breast,
   thinly sliced
3 tbsp sweetcorn kernels
150g tomato salsa
2 large soft flour tortillas
50g Philadelphia Garlic & Herbs,
   softened
green salad, to serve

GENTLY heat the chicken, corn and salsa in a saucepan until warmed through, stirring occasionally.

SPREAD one tortilla with the Philly, spoon over the chicken mixture, then top with the other tortilla.

HEAT a large frying pan to medium–hot and add the filled tortilla. Cook for 2–3 minutes or until golden brown underneath. Turn over with a large spatula and cook the other side until golden brown. Slice into 4 wedges and serve with a green salad.

tip If you prefer, use 4 small soft flour tortillas and fill them with the same quantity of mixture.

Per serving: energy 351kcal, protein 29.8g, carbohydrate 38.1g, fat 9.6g, equivalent as salt 2.0g

roast vegetable ciabatta

serves 6 / prep time 5 minutes / cook time 15–20 minutes

1 red pepper, deseeded
1 yellow pepper, deseeded
1 small red onion, peeled
1 small courgette
1 tbsp olive oil
1 ciabatta loaf
180g Philadelphia Extra Light
salad leaves, to garnish

PREHEAT the oven to 200°C, gas 6. Cut the vegetables into chunks, place in a roasting tin and drizzle with the oil. Roast for about 15–20 minutes or until the vegetables start to brown round the edges.

PREHEAT the grill to High. Cut the ciabatta into 12 slices and lightly toast on both sides under the grill.

SPREAD the ciabatta with the Philly, top with the roasted vegetables, salad leaves and black pepper.

tip Instead of olive oil use a flavoured oil, such as a chilli or garlic oil.

Per serving: energy 200kcal, protein 10.0g, carbohydrate 28.6g, fat 6.2g, equivalent as salt 1.0g

roast pumpkin bruschetta

serves 6 / prep time 10 minutes / cook time 25–30 minutes

1kg pumpkin or butternut squash,
    peeled and deseeded
1 tbsp olive oil
2 sprigs of fresh rosemary
1–2 garlic cloves, finely sliced
1 ciabatta loaf or small white loaf,
    thickly sliced
180g Philadelphia Light

PREHEAT the oven to 200°C, gas 6. Cut the pumpkin or squash into chunks, place in a roasting tin and toss in the oil with the rosemary. Season with black pepper.

BAKE for 15–20 minutes, until golden and tender. Add the garlic and cook for a further 8–10 minutes.

PREHEAT the grill to High. Lightly toast the bread slices on both sides and spread with the Philly. Top with the pumpkin mixture and serve immediately.

tip If you find peeling the pumpkin or squash difficult, try cutting it into chunks first and then cut off the skin.

Per serving: energy 221kcal, protein 8.8g, carbohydrate 31.1g, fat 7.6g, equivalent as salt 1.0g

smoked salmon bruschetta

serves 12 / prep time 5 minutes / cook time 5 minutes

½ medium cucumber, finely chopped
1 tbsp fresh dill, finely chopped
120g Philadelphia Light, softened
zest and juice of ½ lemon
1 ciabatta loaf, cut into 12 slices
125g smoked salmon, sliced

STIR the cucumber and dill into the Philly with the lemon zest and juice. Cover and leave to stand to let the flavours develop whilst you prepare the toast.

PREHEAT the grill to High. Toast the bread on each side until lightly golden and then place a spoonful of the Philly mixture onto each slice of toast.

TOP the Philly mixture with the slices of smoked salmon and season with black pepper.

tip If time allows, prepare the Philly mixture beforehand and pop it in the fridge overnight to let the flavours fully develop.

Per serving: energy 90kcal, protein 5.8g, carbohydrate 11.8g, fat 2.5g, equivalent as salt 0.9g

tuna and olive ciabatta

serves 4 / prep time 5 minutes / cook time 8–10 minutes

1 small ciabatta loaf
120g Philadelphia Extra Light, softened
400g can tuna in spring water, drained
1 tbsp black olives, pitted and halved
a few mixed lettuce leaves

WARM the ciabatta lightly for 5 minutes in a moderate preheated oven. Cut the loaf into 4 pieces, split each in half and spread the bottom halves with the Philly.

ADD the flakes of tuna, olives and mixed lettuce leaves.

TOP with the remaining halves of bread.

tip Alternatively, mix the Philly with the tuna and olives, spread over the ciabatta and add the lettuce leaves just before serving.

Per serving: energy 306kcal, protein 28.5g, carbohydrate 38.1g, fat 5.4g, equivalent as salt 2.2g

chicken tikka bagels

serves 4 / prep time 5 minutes / cook time 2 minutes

4 plain bagels
120g Philadelphia Light, softened
2 tbsp mango chutney
225g cooked chicken tikka, sliced
sprigs of fresh coriander, to garnish

PREHEAT the grill to High. Cut the bagels in half horizontally. Toast until lightly browned on both sides and spread each half with Philly.

SPOON the mango chutney onto the Philly and top with the slices of chicken tikka.

SEASON to taste with black pepper and garnish with sprigs of fresh coriander.

tip Add a little shredded lettuce instead of the fresh coriander or choose a salad leaf mix that contains coriander.

Per serving: energy 347kcal, protein 25.0g, carbohydrate 50.0g, fat 6.4g, equivalent as salt 2.1g

prawn and rocket bagels

serves 4 / prep time 5 minutes / cook time 2 minutes

4 plain bagels
120g Philadelphia Light, softened
125g cooked, peeled prawns
2 tbsp sweet chilli sauce
handful of rocket leaves

PREHEAT the grill to High. Split the bagels in half horizontally. Toast until lightly browned on both sides and spread the bottom halves with the Philly.

STIR the prawns into the sweet chilli sauce and spoon onto the Philly. Add a few rocket leaves to each bagel and top with the other bagel half.

tip Rocket leaves provide a subtle peppery flavour that complements the chilli sauce, but they can be substituted for mixed salad leaves if preferred.

Per serving: energy 308kcal, protein 16.7g, carbohydrate 51.1g, fat 5.0g, equivalent as salt 2.5g

soufflé ramekins

olive oil, for greasing
200g Philadelphia Garlic & Herbs
2 eggs, separated
25g plain flour
1 spring onion, finely sliced
25g mature Cheddar, finely grated

PREHEAT the oven to 190°C, gas 5 and grease
6 individual ramekin dishes. Beat together the Philly,
egg yolks and flour with an electric whisk then stir
in the spring onion and Cheddar.

WHISK the egg whites in a separate bowl until stiff
peaks form. Gently fold through the cheese mixture.
Season to taste.

DIVIDE the mixture between the ramekins and bake
for 12–15 minutes or until golden. Serve immediately.

tip These soufflé ramekins can be made with
Philadelphia Chives, if preferred.

Per serving: energy 123kcal, protein 6.4g, carbohydrate 4.4g, fat 9.0g, equivalent as salt 0.5g

sizzling chicken tortillas

serves 8 / prep time 15 minutes / cook time 10 minutes

1 tbsp sunflower oil
4 boneless, skinless chicken
     breasts, thinly sliced
1 tsp hot chilli powder
1 red and 1 yellow pepper,
     deseeded and thickly sliced
1 red onion, peeled and cut
     into wedges
2 garlic cloves, peeled and
     crushed
120g Philadelphia Light
2 tsp cold water
½ Iceberg lettuce, shredded
4 medium vine tomatoes, sliced
8 soft flour tortillas, warmed
1 ripe avocado, halved, stoned,
     peeled and sliced
lime wedges, for squeezing

HEAT the oil in a large non-stick frying pan. Toss the chicken with the chilli powder and stir-fry for 5–6 minutes until lightly browned and cooked through. Tip the chicken onto a plate and set aside.

ADD the peppers and onion to the pan and stir-fry until softened and lightly browned, adding the garlic for the last minute of cooking time. Then return the chicken to the pan and cook with the vegetables for 2–3 minutes until hot, stirring regularly.

MIX together the Philly and water until it reaches a smooth, dropping consistency. To serve, put some lettuce and a couple of tomato slices onto each tortilla. Top with the cooked chicken and vegetables, then add some sliced avocado and a squeeze of lime. Finish with a couple of teaspoons of the Philly sauce. Roll up and serve immediately.

tips Balance your food choices so you and your family and friends can enjoy a serving of this indulgent recipe as an occasional treat.

Per serving: energy 303kcal, protein 22.7g, carbohydrate 36.8g, fat 11.3g, equivalent as salt 1.8g

classic smoked salmon bagels

serves 4 / prep time 5 minutes / cook time 2 minutes

4 plain or poppy seed bagels
120g Philadelphia Light, softened
75g thinly sliced smoked salmon
a few capers (optional)
juice of ½ lime
fresh dill sprigs, to garnish

PREHEAT the grill to High. Slice the bagels in half horizontally and toast until lightly golden on both sides. Spread the bottom half of each bagel with Philly.

ADD some smoked salmon, a few capers, if using, and squeeze over some lime juice.

FINISH with a little dill, season with black pepper and add the top half of the bagel.

tip Replace the smoked salmon with hot smoked salmon flakes for a more substantial topping.

Per serving: energy 265kcal, protein 14.3g, carbohydrate 41.7g, fat 5.6g, equivalent as salt 2.1g

tuna pittas

serves 4 / prep time 10 minutes

120g Philadelphia Chives
2 spring onions, trimmed and
    sliced thinly into rings
200g can tuna in spring water,
    drained
2 medium tomatoes, sliced
¼ cucumber, thinly sliced
4 wholemeal pitta breads or
    8 mini pittas
1 tbsp chopped fresh chives or fresh
    flatleaf parsley, to garnish

SOFTEN the Philly in a bowl, add the spring onions and flaked tuna and mix together gently to combine.

PLACE the tomato and cucumber slices on the pitta bread and top with the tuna mixture. Garnish with chives or parsley.

Per serving: energy 296kcal, protein 19.3g, carbohydrate 46.6g, fat 4.9g, equivalent as salt 1.5g

creamy hummous wrap

serves 4 / prep time 10 minutes

400g can chickpeas, drained
    and rinsed
120g Philadelphia Light
1 garlic clove
zest of ½ lemon, juice of 1 lemon
4 wraps
50g mixed salad leaves

BLEND the chickpeas with the Philly, garlic, lemon zest and juice and black pepper until smooth. Spread the mixture over the wraps and top with the salad leaves, fold in the edges and roll up tightly. Serve immediately.

Per serving: energy 281kcal, protein 12.6g, carbohydrate 45.6g, fat 6.6g, equivalent as salt 1.3g

savoury bread cases

serves 12 / prep time 10 minutes / cook time 10 minutes

3 slices medium-sliced wholemeal
    bread (from a large loaf)
1 tbsp light olive oil
100g Philadelphia Light
40g diced salmon trimmings
zest of ½ lemon

PREHEAT the oven to 190°C, gas 5. Cut the crusts off the bread and roll the slices with a rolling pin to flatten the bread slightly. Brush each side lightly with oil and cut each slice into 4 to give 12 squares.

PRESS the squares firmly into a 12-hole shallow bun tin and bake in the oven for 8–10 minutes until crisp and golden. Cool and fill each with a dollop of Philly, some smoked salmon and a sprinkle of lemon zest.

tip These bread cases are ideal for parties and can be made a day or two in advance and kept in an airtight container.

Per serving: energy 97kcal, protein 4.9g, carbohydrate 4.8g, fat 6.7g, equivalent as salt 0.7g

chicken salad wrap

serves 2 / prep time 5 minutes / cook time 15 minutes

2 small boneless, skinless
    chicken breasts
2 wraps
60g Philadelphia Extra Light,
    softened
a little (Cos or Iceberg) lettuce
4–5 cherry tomatoes

HEAT the grill to High and pop the chicken under it for 7 minutes each side, or until thoroughly cooked.

SPREAD the wraps with Philly. Slice the lettuce and tomatoes and place on top of the Philly. When cooled slightly, slice and place the grilled chicken on the top and season to taste. Roll up the wraps and enjoy.

tip Use plain wraps or tomato ones for added flavour.

Per serving: energy 342kcal, protein 40.8g, carbohydrate 35g, fat 5.3g, equivalent as salt 0.8g

philly steakwich

serves 1 / prep time 5 minutes / cook time 5 minutes

1 medium seeded sub roll
1 tsp olive oil
1 small red onion, thinly sliced
1 thin frying steak, approx. 100g
25g mushrooms, thinly sliced
30g Philadelphia

PREHEAT the grill to High. Cut the sub roll in half horizontally and toast the halves under the grill, cut side up.

HEAT the oil in a griddle pan or non-stick frying pan and cook the onion for 1 minute before adding the steak and mushrooms. Cook the steak for 1 minute on each side.

SPREAD the Philly over the bottom half of the toasted sub and top with the steak, onion and mushrooms. Top with the other half of the roll and serve.

Per serving: energy 558kcal, protein 35.3g, carbohydrate 47g, fat 25.7g, equivalent as salt 1.0g

philly pan bagnat

serves 6 / prep time 15 minutes, plus firming time

circular country-style loaf
150g Philadelphia Garlic & Herbs
2 cooked chicken breasts, torn
   into pieces
3 tbsp black olive tapenade
large handful of spinach leaves
290g jar roasted vegetables
   (peppers, aubergines, courgettes,
   etc.), drained

CUT the top off the loaf approximately one-quarter of the way down and pull the soft bread out of the centre to make a bowl shape of the crust with a 3cm layer of bread inside. In a separate bowl, mix together the Philly and the chicken until the meat is all coated.

SPREAD the tapenade in a thin layer all over the inside of the bread bowl, layer the spinach leaves over the bottom, then add a layer of chicken, topped with the roasted vegetables. Repeat until the bread bowl is full. Finish with a layer of spinach on top.

REPLACE the loaf lid, tightly wrap the whole thing in cling film and balance a can on top to weight it down. Leave in the fridge to firm up for 1–4 hours. Cut into wedges to serve.

tip Great for picnics, just pack it in its cling film and slice on location.

Per serving: energy 318kcal, protein 22.4g, carbohydrate 36.4g, fat 10.1g, equivalent as salt 1.7g

cucumber rolls / smoked trout and wasabi pastries / thai fish skewers / lettuce bites / caramelised red onion tartlets / chicken and cranberry bites / baked samosas / chicken satay bites / potato skins with guacamole / mexican bean dip / philly feta dip / tzatziki / quick creamy hummous / prawn and cucumber dip / avocado and bacon dip / beetroot dip

PARTY BITES AND DIPS

cucumber rolls

serves 24 / prep time 30–40 minutes / chilling time 20 minutes

2 large cucumbers
200g Philadelphia Light, softened
2 tsp horseradish sauce
2 tsp finely chopped fresh dill, plus
    extra sprigs to garnish
2 tsp finely chopped fresh chives
grated zest of 1 lemon
300g thinly sliced smoked salmon
    or rare roast beef
1 small red pepper, finely sliced into
    5cm lengths or 1 punnet cress,
    trimmed to 5cm lengths

SLICE along the length of the cucumbers using a vegetable peeler, to give 24 slices in total. Pat the slices dry with kitchen paper.

COMBINE the Philly, horseradish, herbs and lemon zest in a small bowl. Spread 2 teaspoons over each cucumber slice (it can be slippery at first). Top the slices with the smoked salmon or beef and trim to fit.

PLACE bundles of red pepper or cress at one end of each slice, then roll up the cucumber to enclose the filling – secure it with cocktail sticks if necessary. Stand upright and refrigerate until the filling is firm. Garnish with dill sprigs.

tip For a special touch, wrap an extra piece of salmon or beef round the cucumber roll and secure with a cocktail stick, then season with salt and black pepper.

Per serving: energy 33kcal, protein 3.8g, carbohydrate 1.2g, fat 1.5g, equivalent as salt 0.5g

smoked trout and wasabi pastries

serves 32 / prep time 30 minutes / cook time 15 minutes

375g pack ready-rolled puff pastry
1 tsp chilli oil
200g Philadelphia, softened
zest and juice of 1 lime
1 tsp wasabi paste
180g smoked trout fillets, cut into
    bite-sized pieces
2 tbsp finely chopped fresh mint
    or fresh coriander, to garnish

PREHEAT the oven to 200°C, gas 6. Brush the pastry evenly with the chilli oil until coated then prick it all over with a fork. Cut into 32 squares and place on baking sheets. Bake for 15 minutes or until golden.

COMBINE the Philly, lime zest and juice and wasabi until smooth.

SPREAD the cooked pastry with the wasabi cream. Top with pieces of trout, garnish with mint or coriander, and season with black pepper.

tip Wasabi has a distinctive, pungent flavour similar to horseradish. If you cannot find wasabi paste use wasabi powder and make it up as per the directions on the packet. Alternatively, stir in a little horseradish sauce to taste.

Per serving: energy 68kcal, protein 2.3g, carbohydrate 4.6g, fat 4.8g, equivalent as salt 0.2g

thai fish skewers

serves 4 / prep time 10 minutes / cook time 12 minutes

350g white fish (haddock,
    cod, whiting, etc.)
1 small green pepper
3 spring onions, trimmed
1 tbsp Thai green curry paste
    (or to taste)
1 tsp cornflour
30g Philadelphia Extra Light

For the dip:
90g Philadelphia Extra Light
¼ cucumber, diced finely

PREHEAT the grill to Medium. Place all of the ingredients for the skewers into a food processor or blender and process to a coarse mixture (do not overprocess).

MOULD the fish mixture onto 8 small wooden skewers to form sausage shapes. Place them under the grill for 10–12 minutes, turning occasionally until browned and the fish has cooked through.

MAKE the dip. Combine the Philly and cucumber and serve with the fish skewers.

tip Soak the wooden skewers in water for 30 minutes prior to use to avoid burning.

Per serving: energy 182kcal, protein 20.6g, carbohydrate 17.0g, fat 3.9g, equivalent as salt 1.0g

lettuce bites

serves 4 / prep time 10 minutes

2 Little Gem lettuce hearts
120g Philadelphia Extra Light
1 medium tomato, seeds removed
    and flesh diced
1 tbsp fresh dill, chopped
50g cooked, peeled prawns,
    roughly chopped

DIVIDE the lettuce into 8 individual leaves, wash and pat dry with kitchen paper.

MIX the Philly with the tomato, dill and some black pepper and place a spoonful onto each leaf. Top with the prawns. Serve.

tip Serve 2 leaves per person as a light lunch or starter or serve as part of a buffet.

Per serving: energy 48kcal, protein 6.1g, carbohydrate 2.4g, fat 1.6g, equivalent as salt 0.3g

caramelised red onion tartlets
serves 20 / prep time 10 minutes / cook time 20 minutes

375g pack ready-rolled puff pastry
80g caramelised red onion chutney
150g Philadelphia Chives

PREHEAT the oven to 200°C, gas 6. Using a 6cm pastry cutter, cut out 20 pastry rounds and use to line the base of 2 greased 12-hole bun tins. Prick the base of the pastry rounds with a fork.

DIVIDE the chutney between the pastry rounds and top each with a spoonful of Philly.

BAKE for about 15–20 minutes until the pastry is puffy and golden. Serve warm.

tip If you like, use Philadelphia Garlic & Herbs in place of the Chives variety.

Per serving: energy 88kcal, protein 1.7g, carbohydrate 8.6g, fat 5.5g, equivalent as salt 0.3g

chicken and cranberry bites
serves 12 / prep time 10 minutes / cook time 15 minutes

375g pack ready-rolled flaky pastry
150g Philadelphia Light
100g cranberry sauce
250g cooked chicken or turkey, cut into pieces

PREHEAT the oven to 220°C, gas 7. Cut the flaky pastry into 24 squares and place on non-stick baking sheets.

SPOON the Philly onto the pastry squares and top with the cranberry sauce and chicken or turkey pieces.

BAKE for 10–15 minutes until the pastry is golden brown. Leave to cool slightly and serve warm.

tip Serve 2 squares per person with a handful of rocket leaves for a lovely starter.

Per serving: energy 196kcal, protein 8.7g, carbohydrate 14.7g, fat 11.9g, equivalent as salt 0.5g

baked samosas

serves 12 / prep time 20 minutes / cook time 12 minutes

1 tbsp olive oil
½ onion, diced
3 tsp ground cumin
200g potatoes, cooked and diced
100g peas
100g Philadelphia Garlic & Herbs
3 sheets filo pastry

PREHEAT the oven to 220°C, gas 7. Heat half the oil in a frying pan and gently cook the onion for 3 minutes until softened. Add the cumin then the cooked potatoes, peas and Philly. Mix well until everything is coated in Philly.

LAY out the filo on a board, long side closest to you, and cut each sheet top to bottom into 4 equally sized strips so you end up with 12 pieces of pastry.

WORKING with 1 piece of pastry at a time and covering the rest with cling film to prevent it drying out, place a teaspoonful of mixture at the bottom left side of the pastry and fold the bottom right corner over it. Continue folding in a triangular fashion until the strip is all rolled up. Brush with the remaining oil and ensure all of the edges are sealed.

REPEAT with the rest of the pastry and mixture then place on a baking sheet and bake for 12–15 minutes until golden.

tip For a meaty version, add some leftover cooked lamb or chicken.

Per serving: energy 58kcal, protein 2.0g, carbohydrate 7.2g, fat 2.6g, equivalent as salt 0.3g

chicken satay bites

serves 4 / prep time 10 minutes, plus 1 hour marinating / cook time 10 minutes

2 boneless, skinless chicken
   breasts, approx. 150g each
1 tbsp light soy sauce
½ tsp dried chilli flakes
100g Philadelphia
2 tbsp crunchy peanut butter

CUT the chicken into long thin strips or cubes. Mix the soy sauce and half the chilli together in a bowl and add the chicken. Marinate for 1 hour.

HEAT the Philly gently in a small saucepan with the peanut butter and remaining chilli flakes to warm through.

PREHEAT the grill to Medium. Thread the chicken onto short wooden skewers and grill for 3–4 minutes until lightly browned and cooked through (when tested with a sharp knife the juices should run clear), turning occasionally. Serve with the Philly satay sauce.

tips Soak wooden skewers for 30 minutes prior to cooking to avoid burning.

Instead of making bite-sized portions, thread lots of chicken onto skewers for a more substantial meal.

Per serving: energy 235kcal, protein 23.1g, carbohydrate 1.3g, fat 15.3g, equivalent as salt 1.0g

potato skins with guacamole

serves 4 / prep time 10 minutes / cook time 15 minutes

4 medium floury potatoes
1 tbsp olive oil
100g Philadelphia Light
1 ripe avocado, peeled and mashed
1 tomato, skinned, deseeded and
   chopped
¼ tsp dried chilli flakes
1 tsp lime zest and 2 tsp lime juice

WASH and prick the potatoes with a sharp knife and cook in the microwave for 8–10 minutes on High until soft (test with a knife to check that they are cooked all the way through). If you don't have a microwave, cook the potatoes in a preheated oven at 190°C, gas 5 for 1 hour or until cooked through.

CUT the cooked potatoes into quarters (lengthways) and scrape out the potato, leaving just a little on the skins. Brush the skins lightly with oil. Grill the skins on both sides until golden brown and crisp.

MIX the Philly with the avocado, tomato, chilli, lime zest and juice and some black pepper. Serve the skins loaded with the guacamole.

tip Combine the scooped-out potato with some fresh or canned salmon and a little Philly to make fish cakes.

Per serving: energy 267kcal, protein 6.6g, carbohydrate 32.5g, fat 13.1g, equivalent as salt 0.3g

mexican bean dip

serves 12 / prep time 15–20 minutes / cook time 5 minutes

200g Philadelphia Extra Light
2 tsp taco seasoning mix
3 soft flour tortillas
200g can refried beans
150g fresh tomato salsa
25g lettuce, shredded (e.g.
    1 Little Gem lettuce)
1 red onion, thinly sliced
2 tbsp black olives, pitted and sliced
1 red pepper and 1 yellow pepper,
    sliced, and 100g sugar snap peas,
    trimmed, to serve

COMBINE the Philly and taco mix. Spread onto the bottom of a serving dish and leave, covered, in the fridge for at least 10 minutes to let the flavours develop. Toast the tortillas on both sides in a dry frying pan until golden and crispy, then slice each into 8 wedges.

LAYER the refried beans, salsa, lettuce, onion and olives on top of the Philly. Serve the dip with the pepper slices, sugar snap peas and tortilla wedges.

tip Sprinkle a little cayenne pepper over the tortillas before frying to add a bit of spiciness and colour.

Per serving: energy 82kcal, protein 4.4g, carbohydrate 12.4g, fat 1.9g, equivalent as salt 0.7g

philly feta dip

serves 10 / prep time 10 minutes / chilling time 20 minutes

200g Philadelphia Extra Light
150g reduced-fat feta, crumbled
2 tbsp lemon juice
½ red onion, finely chopped
1 tbsp fresh mint, finely chopped,
    plus some whole leaves to garnish
4–5 pitta breads, toasted and sliced,
    and 1 large cucumber, cut into
    sticks, to serve

PLACE the Philly, feta and lemon juice in a food processor and mix until smooth. Spoon into a bowl along with the onion and mint. Stir well to combine. Chill for at least 20 minutes before serving to let the flavours develop.

SPOON the mixture into a serving bowl and garnish with whole mint leaves and black pepper.

SERVE alongside the toasted pitta bread and cucumber sticks.

tip If you don't have a food processor you can make a more textured dip by mashing the Philly, lemon juice and feta together with a fork.

Per serving: energy 160kcal, protein 8.4g, carbohydrate 22.9g, fat 4.5g, equivalent as salt 1.2g

tzatziki

serves 6 / prep time 10 minutes

½ cucumber
180g Philadelphia Extra Light
1 garlic clove, crushed
1 tbsp fresh dill, chopped
toasted pitta bread, to serve

CUT the cucumber in half lengthways then scoop out and discard the seeds. Coarsely grate the flesh.

MIX the Philly with the garlic and dill and season. Add the cucumber, mix well and serve with the toasted pitta bread.

Per serving: energy 231kcal, protein 10.9g, carbohydrate 43.9g, fat 2.5g, equivalent as salt 1.3g

quick creamy hummous

serves 6 / prep time 10 minutes

410g can chickpeas, drained and
    rinsed well
100g Philadelphia Extra Light
grated zest and juice of ½ lemon
1–2 garlic cloves
handful of fresh mint leaves
2 warm wholemeal pitta breads,
    to serve
½ green pepper and ½ yellow
    pepper, sliced, 75g radishes,
    7–8 baby plum tomatoes, to serve

PLACE the chickpeas, Philly, lemon zest and juice and garlic in a food processor and process until smooth. Add the black pepper and mint leaves and process again until the mint is finely chopped.

SERVE with the warm pitta bread, peppers, radishes and tomatoes.

Per serving: energy 147kcal, protein 8.3g, carbohydrate 23.6g, fat 3.0g, equivalent as salt 0.7g

prawn and cucumber dip

serves 4 / prep time 10 minutes

50g cooked and peeled prawns,
    roughly chopped
50g cucumber, finely diced
100g Philadelphia Chives
1 tsp lemon juice
toasted pitta bread, to serve

MIX together all of the ingredients and serve with toasted pitta bread cut into triangles.

Per serving: energy 54kcal, protein 5.0g, carbohydrate 1.3g, fat 3.1g, equivalent as salt 0.8g

avocado and bacon dip

serves 4 / prep time 5 minutes / cook time 10 minutes

1 ripe avocado, halved, stoned
    and peeled
100g Philadelphia
1 rasher back bacon, rind and fat
    removed
crusty bread or Melba toast, to serve

MASH the avocado with the Philly and season with black pepper.

PREHEAT the grill to Medium and cook the bacon until really crisp. Allow to cool then crumble it over the avocado. Serve with crusty bread or Melba toast.

Per serving: energy 140kcal, protein 3.4g, carbohydrate 1.5g, fat 13.5g, equivalent as salt 0.5g

beetroot dip

serves 12 / prep time 10–12 minutes / chilling time 15 minutes

150g pickled beetroot, drained
150g Philadelphia Extra Light
a few chopped fresh chives
1 tsp lemon juice and a little zest
½ cucumber, sliced into sticks,
    or seeded crispbread or
    rice crackers, to serve

CHOP 1 beetroot finely. Combine the remaining beetroot in a food processor with the Philly, half the chives, and the lemon zest and juice.

FOLD through the reserved chopped beetroot and place in a serving dish. Chill in the fridge, covered, for about 15 minutes.

GARNISH with the remaining chives and serve with cucumber sticks, seeded crispbread or rice crackers.

tip For a decorative touch, soften a little extra Philly and swirl it through the top of the dip just before serving.

Per serving: energy 20kcal, protein 1.8g, carbohydrate 1.7g, fat 0.6g, equivalent as salt 0.2g

red thai fish curry / plaice with philly, pea and lettuce sauce / plaice with smoked salmon and dill / cod loin with mustard and philly sauce / thai-style sea bass / chive and red pepper fish cakes / griddled swordfish with ginger and lime philly / haddock with pepper and herb topping / fish goujons with tartare sauce / smoked haddock with minted pea sauce / tuna and broccoli bake / smoked haddock and sweet potato pie / garlic and herb salmon / salmon with creamy lentils / tandoori salmon / trout with avocado stuffing / smoked trout and orange salad with philly dressing / salmon en croute / smoked mackerel kedgeree / philly niçoise / grilled prawns with mango salsa / prawn kebabs with herby philly / monkfish with creamy prawns

FISH

red thai fish curry

serves 4 / prep time 10 minutes/ cook time 15 minutes

2 tsp red Thai curry paste
4 tbsp skimmed milk
100g Philadelphia Extra Light
1 red pepper, cut into thin strips
4 spring onions, sliced
2 haddock fillets (approx. 150g
    each), skinned and cut into
    large pieces
150g raw peeled prawns
200g sugar snap peas, halved
100g cooked Thai rice, to serve
1 lime, cut into wedges, to serve
25g fresh coriander leaves,
    roughly chopped

OVER a low heat, fry the red Thai curry paste in a large saucepan for about 1 minute. Add the milk and Philly, continuing to cook gently. When the Philly has melted, stir in the red pepper and cook for a few minutes.

ADD the spring onions, fish, prawns and sugar snap peas. Leave to cook for about 5 minutes until the prawns have turned pink and the fish flakes easily.

SERVE straight away with the rice, a squeeze of lime juice and a scattering of coriander.

tip Red Thai curry paste can be spicy, so you could swap it for the green version, which is usually milder, if you prefer.

Per serving: energy 251kcal, protein 28.6g, carbohydrate 27.3g, fat 2.9g, equivalent as salt 0.7g

plaice with philly, pea and lettuce sauce

serves 4 / prep time 15 minutes / cook time 10 minutes

4 spring onions, sliced
25g butter
450g frozen peas, defrosted
100g Philadelphia Light
125ml vegetable stock (ideally
    reduced-salt)
1 Little Gem lettuce, shredded
1 tsp caster sugar
8 plaice fillets, skinned, approx.
    100g each
juice of 1 lemon
1 tbsp fresh mint leaves

SOFTEN the spring onions in the butter for
3–4 minutes in a saucepan over a gentle heat.
Tip in the peas and add the Philly to heat through.
Add in enough of the stock to make a creamy sauce.
Add the shredded lettuce and sugar and simmer
for 3–4 minutes. You might need to add a dash
more stock.

WHILE the sauce is cooking, roll up the fish fillets
and secure each one with a cocktail stick. Squeeze
the lemon juice over the fillets, then steam for about
6–8 minutes until tender. (If you don't have a steamer
you can set a colander above a pan of simmering
water and cover it with a lid.)

REMOVE the fillets from the steamer and serve with
the warmed sauce. Scatter with the whole mint leaves
before serving.

Per serving: energy 329kcal, protein 42.3g, carbohydrate 13.0g, fat 12.0g, equivalent as salt 1.2g

plaice with smoked salmon and dill

serves 4 / prep time 10 minutes / cook time 10 minutes

100g Philadelphia
1 tbsp chopped fresh dill
50g smoked salmon, diced
4 skinless plaice fillets, approx.
   125g each

MIX together the Philly, dill and smoked salmon with some black pepper in a bowl.

LAY the plaice fillets on a board and divide the salmon mixture between them. Roll up the fish and secure with a cocktail stick.

PLACE in a steamer and cook for 8–10 minutes until the fish flakes when tested with a knife. (If you don't have a steamer you can set a colander above a pan of simmering water and cover it with a lid.)

tip Delicious served with a selection of steamed vegetables.

Per serving: energy 195kcal, protein 26.0g, carbohydrate 0.0g, fat 10.2g, equivalent as salt 1.3g

cod loin with mustard and philly sauce

serves 2 / prep time 10 minutes / cook time 7 minutes

300g cod loin, cut in half
60g Philadelphia Extra Light
1 tbsp Dijon mustard
1 tsp wholegrain mustard
2 tbsp milk

STEAM the cod for 5 minutes or until cooked (the fish should flake when tested with a knife).

HEAT the Philly gently in a small pan with the mustards and milk, being careful not to let it boil.

SERVE the cod with the mustard sauce.

Per serving: energy 181kcal, protein 32.7g, carbohydrate 3.4g, fat 4.1g, equivalent as salt 1.5g

thai-style sea bass

serves 4 / prep time 20 minutes / cook time 15–20 minutes

4 sea bass fillets, each cut
  lengthways into 3
1½ tbsp sunflower oil
noodles and stir-fried vegetables,
  to serve

For the marinade:
½ tsp fennel seeds
½ tsp coriander seeds
½ tsp dried chilli flakes
1 garlic clove, crushed
1 tbsp Thai fish sauce
2 tsp olive oil
pinch of sugar

For the dressing:
100g Philadelphia Light
zest and juice of 1 lime
1 tbsp chopped fresh coriander
¼ tsp dried chilli flakes
2 tsp olive oil

PLACE all of the dry marinade ingredients into a pestle and mortar and grind well to release the flavours. Stir in the fish sauce and oil. Pour over the sea bass fillets and leave for 15 minutes to marinate.

COMBINE the dressing ingredients and warm gently in a small pan, but do not let it boil. Put to one side while the fish cooks.

HEAT the oil in a frying pan and fry the sea bass fillets skin-side down for 2 minutes, then turn over and cook for a further minute. Serve the fish with the dressing spooned over on a bed of noodles and stir-fried vegetables.

tip If you don't have a pestle and mortar, place the ingredients in a sturdy bowl and use the end of a rolling pin to crush them.

Per serving: energy 246kcal, protein 31.4g, carbohydrate 2.7g, fat 12.3g, equivalent as salt 0.9g

chive and red pepper fish cakes

serves 4 / prep time 20 minutes / cook time 15 minutes

15g butter
1 onion, finely chopped
½ red pepper, finely chopped
400g white fish (e.g. haddock, whiting, coley), minced or finely chopped
50g Philadelphia Chives, softened
100g fresh breadcrumbs
2 tbsp chopped fresh chives
½ tsp paprika
1 tsp garlic powder (optional)
plain flour, for coating
sunflower oil, for shallow frying

MELT the butter and sauté the onion and pepper for 3–5 minutes. Allow to cool then stir in the fish, Philly, breadcrumbs, chives, paprika and garlic, if using. Mix together well.

FORM the mixture into 4 patties, toss in a little flour to coat, and refrigerate until firm.

HEAT a little oil in a frying pan and cook the fish cakes for about 8–10 minutes, turning once, until golden and cooked through. Place on kitchen paper to soak up any excess oil. Serve immediately.

tip For a delicious meal idea, serve the fish cakes with potato or vegetable wedges, salad, a spoonful of creamy caper sauce (see page 99) and a slice of lemon.

Per serving: energy 301kcal, protein 28.7g, carbohydrate 25.5g, fat 10.1g, equivalent as salt 1.7g

griddled swordfish with ginger and lime philly

serves 4 / prep time 15 minutes / cook time 10 minutes

4 swordfish steaks, approx.
    150g each
120g Philadelphia Extra Light
2.5cm piece of fresh root ginger,
    peeled and very finely chopped
finely grated rind of ½ lime, plus
    wedges to serve
1 tbsp chopped fresh coriander
200g Tenderstem broccoli, to serve

GRIDDLE or barbecue the swordfish for approximately 6–8 minutes, turning once, until just cooked through.

MIX together all of the remaining ingredients, except the broccoli, and serve the swordfish with a spoonful of the Philly mixture on top. (Alternatively, gently heat the Philly cream and serve as a sauce with the fish.)

SERVE with steamed Tenderstem broccoli and a wedge of lime.

tip Salmon steaks or fillets can be used in place of the swordfish, if preferred.

Per serving: energy 199kcal, protein 30.7g, carbohydrate 1.8g, fat 7.6g, equivalent as salt 0.8g

haddock with pepper and herb topping

serves 4 / prep time 10 minutes / cook time 20 minutes

2 large haddock fillets, skin
   removed (approx. 180g each)
½ red pepper, deseeded
½ orange pepper, deseeded
120g Philadelphia Extra Light
1 tbsp chopped fresh thyme
500g spinach leaves, washed

PREHEAT the oven to 190°C, gas 5. Place the haddock in an ovenproof dish. Finely chop the peppers and stir them into the Philly with the thyme and some black pepper until combined. Top the haddock with this mixture then bake in the oven for 20–25 minutes until the fish is cooked through.

PLACE the washed spinach in a large saucepan with a tightly fitting lid and cook on a low heat for several minutes until just wilted. Drain well and serve with the haddock on top.

tip Alternatively, serve baby spinach leaves raw as a salad.

Per serving: energy 173kcal, protein 29.4g, carbohydrate 6.3g, fat 3.3g, equivalent as salt 1.0g

fish goujons with tartare sauce

serves 4 / prep time 10 minutes / cook time 15 minutes

300g firm white fish fillets,
   (e.g. haddock, whiting, coley)
1 tsp paprika
30g Philadelphia Chives
50g wholemeal breadcrumbs

For the sauce:
90g Philadelphia Chives
2 tsp capers, chopped
1 tbsp chopped gherkins

PREHEAT the oven to 200°C, gas 6 or the grill to Medium, if you prefer. Cut the fish into strips and dust with paprika. Spread thinly with Philly then coat in the breadcrumbs. Place on a baking sheet and cook in the oven for 12–15 minutes until golden, or grill for 8 minutes, turning occasionally.

MIX together the sauce ingredients and serve alongside the goujons.

Per serving: energy 157kcal, protein 18.5g, carbohydrate 11.4g, fat 4.4g, equivalent as salt 1.0g

smoked haddock with minted pea sauce

serves 2 / prep time 10 minutes / cook time 10 minutes

2 pieces undyed smoked haddock,
    approx. 150g each
100g frozen peas
1 tsp fresh mint, chopped
60g Philadelphia Light
seasonal vegetables, to serve

STEAM or poach the haddock for 5–7 minutes until the fish flakes when tested with a knife. Cook the peas for 1–2 minutes in a saucepan of boiling water, drain, and purée with the mint and Philly using a hand blender or liquidiser.

SEASON with black pepper to taste.

SPOON the sauce onto the plates, spreading it out slightly in a circle and place the fish on top. Serve with seasonal vegetables.

Per serving: energy 201kcal, protein 33.9g, carbohydrate 5.9g, fat 4.8g, equivalent as salt 3.3g

tuna and broccoli bake

serves 4 / prep time 10 minutes / cook time 10 minutes

300g broccoli florets
200g can tuna in spring water,
    drained and flaked
120g Philadelphia
125ml milk
zest of ½ lemon (the remainder
    of the lemon can be served
    with the bake)
1 tbsp chopped fresh flatleaf
    parsley
25g breadcrumbs
1 garlic clove, crushed

PREHEAT the oven to 190°C, gas 5. Cook the broccoli until tender in a saucepan of boiling water and drain well. Place in a large ovenproof dish with the tuna.

GENTLY heat the Philly and milk in a pan over a low heat until the Philly has melted, then add the lemon zest and parsley. Pour the sauce over the broccoli and tuna. Mix the breadcrumbs with the garlic, sprinkle over the top of the tuna and bake in the oven for 10 minutes until lightly browned.

Per serving: energy 201kcal, protein 18.0g, carbohydrate 7.9g, fat 11.0g, equivalent as salt 0.8g

smoked haddock and sweet potato pie

serves 4 / prep time 15 minutes / cook time 35–40 minutes

1kg sweet potatoes, peeled and
    cut into 3cm cubes
120g Philadelphia Chives
300g undyed smoked haddock
300g haddock loin
2 tbsp milk

PREHEAT the oven to 190°C, gas 5. In a large saucepan, cover the potatoes with water, bring to the boil and cook for approximately 10 minutes or until soft. Drain well and mash with 20g of the Philly. Set aside.

PLACE the fish in a microwaveable dish with a teaspoon of the milk, cover and microwave on High for approximately 5 minutes, or steam for 8–10 minutes until just cooked. Remove the skin and any bones, flake the fish and place in a large ovenproof dish.

COMBINE the remaining Philly and milk and spoon over the fish. Top with the mashed sweet potato and bake for 20 minutes until the Philly sauce is bubbling around the edge of the dish and the potato is browned.

tip The sweet potato adds a great splash of colour but you can make this with ordinary mashed potato too.

Per serving: energy 390kcal, protein 34.3g, carbohydrate 54.9g, fat 5.4g, equivalent as salt 2.2g

garlic and herb salmon

serves 4 · prep time 10 minutes · cook time 15–20 minutes

50g white bread
a few fresh chives, chopped
zest of 1 lemon
4 salmon fillets
olive oil for greasing
100g Philadelphia Garlic & Herbs
new potatoes and salad leaves or
    a bunch of watercress, to serve

PREHEAT the oven to 180°C, gas 4. Place the bread in a food processor and blend to fine breadcrumbs. Stir in the chives and lemon zest.

SPREAD the salmon fillets with a thick layer of Philly and place on a lightly oiled baking sheet.

TOP with the flavoured breadcrumbs, lightly pressing them into the Philly. Roast in the oven for 15–20 minutes or until cooked. Serve the salmon with new potatoes and salad leaves or watercress.

tip if the fish is a little wet, pat it dry with kitchen paper or dust it with flour so that it is easier to spread the Philly over it without it sliding off.

Per serving: energy 358kcal, protein 25.4g, carbohydrate 30.6g, fat 15.7g, equivalent as salt 0.3g

salmon with creamy lentils

serves 4 / prep time 5 minutes / cook time 20 minutes

225g Pardina or Puy lentils
400ml vegetable stock
100ml white wine
4 salmon fillets, approx. 150g each
120g Philadelphia Light

PREHEAT the oven to 200°C, gas 6. Rinse the lentils then simmer them in a saucepan with the stock and wine for 20 minutes until tender. Halfway through cooking, place the salmon in the oven for 10–12 minutes until cooked (the fish should flake when tested with a knife).

STIR the Philly and black pepper into the lentils until melted. Spoon onto 4 plates and top with the salmon.

Per serving: energy 506kcal, protein 46.7g, carbohydrate 29.6g, fat 21.3g, equivalent as salt 1.3g

tandoori salmon

serves 2 / prep time 15 minutes / cook time 15 minutes

50g Philadelphia Light
4 tsp tandoori paste
2 boneless salmon fillets,
    approx. 150g each
100g couscous
50g sugar snap peas, cut into pieces
50g baby corn, cut into pieces

MIX together the Philly and tandoori paste in a bowl.

CUT the salmon into chunks and coat well with the Philly mixture. Leave to marinate for 5–10 minutes.

PREHEAT the grill to Medium. Carefully thread the chunks of salmon onto skewers and grill for 8–10 minutes until the fish is cooked through.

MEANWHILE, make up the couscous according to the packet instructions and steam the vegetables. Serve with the salmon.

tips Alternatively, coat whole salmon fillets with the paste, leave to marinate, then grill for 6–8 minutes on each side until the fish is cooked through. The fish will take on a slightly blackened appearance, which is the nature of tandoori.

Per serving: energy 479kcal, protein 38.8g, carbohydrate 27.8g, fat 24.0g, equivalent as salt 1.3g

trout with avocado stuffing

serves 2 / prep time 10–12 minutes / cook time 20–25 minutes

2 whole trout, cleaned
olive oil for greasing
juice of ½ lemon
seasonal vegetables, to serve

For the stuffing:
½ ripe avocado, halved, peeled,
    stoned and diced
4 cherry tomatoes, quartered
60g Philadelphia Garlic & Herbs

PREHEAT the oven to 190°C, gas 5. Mix together the stuffing ingredients.

FILL the trout cavity with the stuffing and place in an oiled ovenproof dish. Pour over the lemon juice.

BAKE for 20–25 minutes until the fish is cooked and flakes easily. Serve with seasonal vegetables.

tip Whole trout are available from major supermarkets or your local fishmonger and they will clean the fish for you, if required.

Per serving: energy 358kcal, protein 25.4g, carbohydrate 30.6g, fat 15.7g, equivalent as salt 0.3g

smoked trout and orange salad with philly dressing

serves 2 / prep time 10 minutes

1 smoked trout fillet,
    approx. 50–75g
1 orange
50g Philadelphia Extra Light
1 tbsp chopped fresh dill
mixed salad leaves

DIVIDE the trout into large flakes. Grate the rind of approximately one-quarter of the orange and set aside the zest. Cut the rind off the orange and chop the flesh into segments, reserving any juice for the dressing.

IN a bowl, mix together the Philly, orange zest, 1–2 tablespoons orange juice, dill and some black pepper.

PLACE the salad leaves on 2 plates, top with the flaked trout and orange segments and drizzle over the Philly and dill dressing.

tips Try using red grapefruit in place of the orange, or use smoked mackerel instead of trout.

To reduce the salt content, replace the smoked trout with poached salmon flakes.

Per serving: energy 114kcal, protein 12.6g, carbohydrate 8.2g, fat 3.9g, equivalent as salt 1.5g

salmon en croûte

serves 2 / prep time 15 minutes / cook time 25–30 minutes

60g Philadelphia Garlic & Herbs
1 tbsp milk
2 tsp lemon juice
150g puff pastry, thawed if frozen
2 salmon fillets, skinned
1 egg, beaten
green salad or steamed vegetables,
    to serve

PREHEAT the oven to 200°C, gas 6. Blend the Philly, milk and lemon juice together with some black pepper.

ROLL out the pastry and cut into 4 oblongs to fit the size of the salmon fillets. Place the fillets on 2 of the pastry pieces and spoon the Philly mixture onto the salmon. Brush the edges of the pastry with beaten egg, top with the remaining pastry oblongs and seal the edges together.

BRUSH the top of the salmon parcels with the remaining egg and bake for 25–30 minutes until golden brown. Serve immediately with a green salad or steamed vegetables.

tip You can also make this using Philadelphia Light and mix in your favourite chopped fresh leafy herbs, e.g. basil, parsley or coriander.

Per serving: energy 704kcal, protein 44.0g, carbohydrate 34.4g, fat 45.5g, equivalent as salt 1.4g

smoked mackerel kedgeree

serves 4 / prep time 10 minutes / cook time 15 minutes

200g basmati rice
1 tsp olive oil
1 small onion, finely chopped
100g smoked mackerel, flaked
120g Philadelphia Light
1 tbsp milk
1 tbsp chopped fresh flatleaf parsley
grated zest and juice of ½ lemon
2 hard-boiled eggs, quartered

COOK the rice in a pan of boiling water for 10–12 minutes until cooked. Drain well.

HEAT the oil in a frying pan and fry the onion for 1 minute until soft. Add the mackerel and heat for 1 minute. Turn off the heat and add the Philly with the milk, parsley and lemon zest and juice until the Philly has melted. Stir in the rice, mix, then tip out onto a serving dish and garnish with the hard-boiled eggs.

Per serving: energy 383kcal, protein 15.2g, carbohydrate 42.7g, fat 16.5g, equivalent as salt 1.0g

philly niçoise

200g new potatoes
100g asparagus
2 medium tuna steaks
1 tsp olive oil
50g Philadelphia Chives
3–4 tbsp milk
4 medium tomatoes, quartered
50g black olives, pitted and halved
25g watercress

PLACE the new potatoes in a saucepan of water, bring to the boil and cook until tender.

PREHEAT a griddle pan. Brush the asparagus and tuna with the oil and pop them onto the griddle and cook for 3–4 minutes until browned. Turn over and continue cooking until browned on the other side.

MELT the Philly and milk in a small saucepan over a low heat until smooth.

QUARTER the cooked new potatoes and place them on a serving plate with the tomatoes, olives, watercress and asparagus. Top with the tuna and drizzle over the warm Philly dressing.

tip Tuna should ideally be eaten medium-rare, but if you prefer your tuna cooked all the way through, leave it on the griddle for a few more minutes. Be careful not to overcook the fish, though, or it will quickly dry out.

Per serving: energy 395kcal, protein 40.3g, carbohydrate 25.8g, fat 15.3g, equivalent as salt 2.0g

grilled prawns with mango salsa

serves 4 / prep time 20–25 minutes, including marinating / cook time 8–10 minutes

100g Philadelphia Light
zest and juice of 1 lime
1 fresh red chilli, deseeded
    and finely chopped
24 tail-on cooked king prawns

For the salsa:
1 ripe mango, peeled, stoned
    and diced
½ red onion, finely chopped
1 tbsp chopped fresh coriander
juice of 1 lime
1 small bag of salad leaves

PREHEAT the grill to Medium. In a bowl, mix the Philly, zest and juice of the lime and half the chilli. Add the prawns and mix well to coat. Leave to marinate for 20 minutes.

MIX together the salsa ingredients and the remaining chilli and leave on one side.

THREAD the prawns onto 8 skewers and grill for approximately 4–5 minutes, turning occasionally, until lightly browned. Serve with the salsa and some salad leaves.

tip To make this recipe with uncooked prawns, thread them onto the skewers and cook for about 8 minutes until they turn pink all over.

Per serving: energy 121kcal, protein 14.1g, carbohydrate 8.4g, fat 3.6g, equivalent as salt 2.2g

prawn kebabs with herby philly

serves 4 / prep time 20 minutes / cook time 5 minutes

12 large raw prawns, peeled but
   with tail left on
1 tsp olive oil
120g Philadelphia Garlic & Herbs
1 tbsp chopped mixed fresh herbs
   (e.g. chives, parsley, dill)
1 bunch of fresh lemon thyme,
   for steaming

WITH a sharp knife, remove the black intestine from the back of the prawns. Place the prawns onto 4 skewers and brush with the oil.

MIX the Philly with the herbs and some black pepper. Steam the prawns in a steamer on a bed of lemon thyme for 3–4 minutes until they have turned pink. Serve with the dip.

Per serving: energy 79kcal, protein 6.4g, carbohydrate 1.0g, fat 5.6g, equivalent as salt 0.5g

monkfish with creamy prawns

serves 2 / prep time 10 minutes / cook time 15 minutes

2 monkfish tail fillets, approx.
    150g each in weight
60g Philadelphia Light
50g peeled, raw tiger prawns,
    roughly chopped
zest of ½ lemon (use the juice to
    squeeze over the fish)
1 tbsp chopped fresh flatleaf parsley
seasonal vegetables, to serve

PREHEAT the oven to 190°C, gas 5. Place the fish on a non-stick baking sheet. Mix the Philly with the prawns, lemon zest, parsley and some black pepper and place on top of the fish. Bake in the oven for 10–15 minutes until the fish flakes when tested with a knife.

SQUEEZE over the lemon juice and serve with seasonal vegetables.

tip This works well with haddock or cod loin, too.

Per serving: energy 163kcal, protein 29.9g, carbohydrate 1.3g, fat 4.3g, equivalent as salt 0.8g

garlic and herb philly-stuffed chicken / creamy spanish chicken pie / philly chicken and parma ham / chicken and leek pie with philly / tex mex chicken with philly guacamole / thai green chicken curry / chicken goujons / chicken with salsa verde / chilli philly chicken / coriander and lime chicken / spicy chicken tacos with mango rice / apricot and almond chicken / philly and ginger chicken with lemon rice / chicken, porcini and sweet marsala sauce / stir-fried chicken tortillas / chicken biryani / roast aubergine and chicken curry / chicken and nectarine salad / chinese chicken salad

CHICKEN

garlic and herb philly-stuffed chicken

serves 6 / prep time 15 minutes / cook time 2 hours 10 minutes

1 onion, grated
100g breadcrumbs
1 lemon
120g Philadelphia Garlic & Herbs
large chicken, approx. 2.5kg

PREHEAT the oven to 180°C, gas 4. In a bowl, mix together the onion, breadcrumbs, zest of the lemon and the Philly.

WITH the chicken legs pointing towards you, work your fingers under the chicken skin to separate it from the breast. Take care not to tear the skin. Work dollops of the stuffing up under the skin, spreading it out so it covers the entire breast area; pull the skin back into place and secure with a skewer or some cocktail sticks.

CUT the now zestless lemon in half, give it a squeeze and tuck it inside the chicken cavity. Cook the chicken for 2 hours 10 minutes. After 30 minutes gently turn it onto one side, and after another 30 minutes turn it over onto the other side, then back to upright for the remaining time.

CHECK that the bird is cooked through; none of the meat should be pink and when you pierce the thickest part of the chicken flesh with a skewer or the point of a sharp knife, the juices should run clear.

Per serving: energy 493kcal, protein 32.6g, carbohydrate 18.7g, fat 32.5g, equivalent as salt 1.0g

creamy spanish chicken pie

serves 6 / prep time 15 minutes / cook time 20 minutes

1kg floury potatoes, cut into quarters
290g jar roasted vegetables in oil, drained then chopped into bite-sized pieces, oil reserved
2 onions, diced
1 garlic clove, finely diced
2 x 400g cans tomatoes
1 tsp smoked paprika
150g Philadelphia Extra Light
300g cooked chicken, shredded into pieces

PREHEAT the oven to 180°C, gas 4. Boil the potatoes in a saucepan of salted water for 15 minutes until tender.

WHILE they are cooking, heat a drizzle of the oil from the roasted vegetables in a frying pan, add the onions, fry gently for 5 minutes then add the garlic and cook for a further 2 minutes. Tip in the tomatoes and paprika, stir well and bring to a simmer.

ONCE the potatoes are cooked, drain them, then add the Philly and mash together. Tip the tomatoes, chicken and roasted vegetables into a large ovenproof dish and mix.

TOP the chicken mixture with the creamy mashed potato and rough up the top slightly with a fork. Cook for 20 minutes until piping hot all the way through.

tip Use chicken left over from a roast or cook it for the recipe.

Per serving: energy 235kcal, protein 3.7g, carbohydrate 28.3g, fat 7.2g, equivalent as salt 0.5g

philly chicken and parma ham

serves 4 / prep time 10 minutes / cook time 25 minutes

4 boneless, skinless chicken
   breasts
120g Philadelphia Basil
8 slices Parma ham
1 stern of vine-ripened tomatoes
   (6–8 tomatoes)
mixed salad leaves

PREHEAT the oven to 200°C, gas 6. Split the chicken breasts down the middle, making a pocket in each, and spoon in the Philly. Close the pocket then wrap each chicken breast in 2 slices of Parma ham.

PLACE the chicken in a non-stick ovenproof dish and bake for 20–25 minutes until the chicken is thoroughly cooked and the juices run clear when the meat is tested with a skewer.

AFTER 10 minutes, put the tomatoes on a baking sheet and put it in the oven, cooking them for 10–15 minutes. Leave to cool slightly then cut the chicken in half to expose the melted Philly. Serve with some mixed salad leaves and the tomatoes.

tip You could also use Philadelphia Chives in this recipe, for a change.

Per serving: energy 258kcal, protein 40.7g, carbohydrate 6.3g, fat 7.9g, equivalent as salt 1.5g

chicken and leek pie with philly

serves 6 / prep time 40 minutes / cook time 30–35 minutes

2 tbsp olive oil, plus extra for greasing

4 boneless, skinless chicken breasts, cubed, or 375g leftover cooked chicken

1 tsp butter

3 leeks, washed and cut into 1cm-thick rounds

1 tbsp plain flour

125ml white wine

200ml chicken stock (use reduced-salt if you like)

100g Philadelphia Light

1 tbsp chopped fresh flatleaf parsley

2 sheets filo pastry

PREHEAT the oven to 190°C, gas 5. Heat the oil in a frying pan and cook the raw chicken for about 5–10 minutes until tender, stirring often. Remove from the pan and set aside. (Omit this step if you are using cooked chicken.)

ADD the butter to the pan and soften the leeks, without colouring, for 5 minutes. Sprinkle over the flour and cook, stirring all the time, for a further 2 minutes. Stir in the wine and chicken stock, bring to a simmer and cook for about 5 minutes until lightly thickened. Add the Philly and stir until it has melted. Add a dash of water if the sauce looks too thick.

RETURN the chicken to the pan and add the parsley. Spoon the mixture into a shallow, 1-litre ovenproof pie dish and leave to cool.

BRUSH the edge of the pie dish with oil. Lay a sheet of pastry over the pie dish. Brush with oil, then repeat with the other sheet. Scrunch up the overhanging pastry, fold it onto the pie's surface, and brush with more oil.

BAKE in the oven for 30–35 minutes until golden. Serve straight from the dish.

tip Sprinkle sesame or poppy seeds on top of the filo pastry before cooking.

Per serving: energy 249kcal, protein 26.2g, carbohydrate 11.8g, fat 9.5g, equivalent as salt 0.7g

tex-mex chicken with philly guacamole

serves 4 / prep time 10 minutes / cook time 10 minutes

4 boneless, skinless chicken breasts
2 garlic cloves, crushed
2 limes
1 avocado
1 fresh red chilli, finely diced
100g Philadelphia Chives

CUT each chicken breast in half horizontally so you end up with 2 flat pieces of chicken. Mix half the garlic with the juice and zest of 1 lime and rub the mixture over the chicken pieces. Set aside to marinate.

STONE and skin the avocado and mash in a small bowl, then add the chilli, the remaining garlic, Philly and the juice of the remaining lime. Stir well.

GRILL, griddle or barbecue the chicken for 2–3 minutes on each side until cooked through and serve with a dollop of the guacamole.

tip Use the Philly guacamole as a dip or serve with nachos and cheese.

Per serving: energy 251kcal, protein 34.3g, carbohydrate 2.4g, fat 11.5g, equivalent as salt 0.5g

thai green chicken curry

serves 4 / prep time 10 minutes / cook time 20 minutes

2 tsp Thai green curry paste
4 boneless, skinless chicken
    breasts, cut into pieces
1 small onion, finely sliced
1 green pepper, finely sliced
1 red pepper, finely sliced
120g Philadelphia Extra Light
3–4 tbsp skimmed milk
steamed Thai rice, to serve
fresh coriander leaves, to garnish

HEAT a large non-stick saucepan and add the Thai curry paste, chicken and onion. Fry on a medium heat for 6–8 minutes until the chicken is cooked through.

ADD the peppers to the pan and continue cooking for 3–4 minutes until they have softened and the chicken is golden brown.

STIR the Philly and milk through the mixture until melted. Serve with the steamed Thai rice and garnish with some coriander leaves.

tip The heat of curry pastes can vary, so check it before you use it. You can always add a little more if you like a hotter curry.

Per serving: energy 265kcal, protein 46.8g, carbohydrate 7.2g, fat 5.6g, equivalent as salt 0.7g

chicken goujons

serves 2 / prep time 10 minutes / cook time 20 minutes

50g wholemeal bread
15g chopped hazelnuts
50g Philadelphia Chives
238g pack mini chicken breast
    fillets (approx. 8)
25g sweet chilli sauce, to serve
a few salad leaves, to garnish

PREHEAT the oven to 200°C, gas 6. Place the bread in a food processor and whizz to make fine breadcrumbs. Add the nuts and process again to blend them together.

SPREAD the Philly evenly over the surface of the chicken pieces and coat them well with the breadcrumb mixture. Place onto a lightly oiled baking sheet and cook in the oven for 15–20 minutes until golden and the chicken is firm to the touch. Serve with the sweet chilli sauce on the side for dipping and the salad leaves.

Per serving: energy 351kcal, protein 44.7g, carbohydrate 15.3g, fat 12.6g, equivalent as salt 1.5g

chicken with salsa verde

serves 4 / prep time 15 minutes / cook time 25 minutes

4 boneless, skinless chicken breasts
120g Philadelphia, softened
4 anchovies, roughly chopped
2 tbsp finely chopped fresh
    flatleaf parsley
2 tbsp roughly chopped capers
8 baby spinach leaves
2 tsp olive oil

For the salsa verde:
50ml olive oil
2 tbsp finely chopped fresh
    flatleaf parsley
2 tbsp finely chopped fresh basil
1 tbsp white wine vinegar
1 tbsp finely chopped pitted
    green olives
1 tbsp finely chopped capers
1 tbsp finely chopped gherkins
3 anchovies, finely chopped
1 garlic clove, crushed

PREHEAT the oven to 180°C, gas 4. Cut a long deep slit in one side of each chicken breast to make a pocket. Mix together the Philly, anchovies, parsley and capers. Stuff each chicken breast with one quarter of the Philly mixture and top with spinach leaves. Close and seal with wooden cocktail sticks.

RUB a little oil over the chicken breasts. Transfer the chicken to a roasting tin and cook in the oven for about 25 minutes or until the chicken is cooked and the juices run clear when tested with a skewer.

COMBINE all the salsa verde ingredients in a bowl and spoon over the chicken to serve.

tip For a quicker version, spoon a little pesto over the chicken instead of making the salsa verde.

Per serving: energy 432kcal, protein 48.3g, carbohydrate 1.5g, fat 25.9g, equivalent as salt 1.4g

chilli philly chicken

serves 4 / prep time 10 minutes / cook time 25 minutes

4 large mild fresh green chillies
4 garlic cloves
5cm piece of fresh root ginger
120g Philadelphia Garlic & Herbs
1 tbsp nut or vegetable oil
8 boneless, skinless chicken thighs
1 onion, peeled and thinly sliced
600ml chicken stock
cooked basmati rice, to serve
fresh coriander leaves, to serve

CUT the chillies open, remove the seeds and stalks, then chop into chunks. Peel and roughly chop the garlic and ginger then drop them all into a food processor along with the Philly and blitz until you get a smooth paste. Stop and scrape down the sides of the food processor bowl with a spatula, if needed.

HEAT the oil in a frying pan, add the chicken and cook on all sides until golden. Add the onion and continue cooking until it is soft and colouring.

ADD the Philly mixture and stock and stir well. Reduce the heat and simmer gently for 15 minutes until the sauce is thick and the chicken is cooked through. Serve with basmati rice and coriander leaves stirred through.

tip If you like your food hotter, swap the green chillies for more fiery red ones.

Per serving: energy 326kcal, protein 7.5g, carbohydrate 58.5g, fat 8.4g, equivalent as salt 1.0g

coriander and lime chicken

serves 4 / prep time 10 minutes / cook time 15 minutes

4 boneless, skinless chicken breasts
100g Philadelphia Light
zest and juice of 2 limes, plus wedges
    to serve (optional)
2 garlic cloves, crushed
3 tbsp chopped fresh coriander
mixed salad leaves
2 mixed peppers, sliced

PREHEAT the grill to Medium–Hot. Make 3 or 4 deep cuts in the surface of the chicken breasts.

MIX together the Philly, lime zest and juice, garlic and coriander in a large bowl. Add the chicken and coat well. Cook under the grill for 12–15 minutes, turning once, until the juices of the chicken run clear when tested with a skewer.

SERVE with salad, mixed peppers and a wedge of lime, if liked.

tip The chicken can also be cooked on a barbecue.

Per serving: energy 260kcal, protein 44.7g, carbohydrate 6.2g, fat 6.1g, equivalent as salt 0.5g

spicy chicken tacos
with mango rice

serves 2 / prep time 10 minutes / cook time 15 minutes

100g wild rice
200g chicken pieces
3 tsp fajita seasoning
2 tsp vegetable oil
1 small red pepper, cut into chunks
1 small ripe mango, peeled, stoned and cut into small chunks
4 taco shells
60g Philadelphia Garlic & Herbs

HEAT the oven to 150°C, gas 2. Cook the rice according to the packet instructions.

TOSS the chicken pieces in 2 teaspoons of the fajita seasoning. Heat the oil in a frying pan and cook the chicken for 5 minutes until browned on all sides, add the pepper and a quarter of the mango.

HEAT the taco shells in the oven for 5 minutes. Beat the Philly in a bowl until it loosens and add the remaining fajita seasoning, mixing well. Stir the rest of the mango into the rice and divide it between 2 plates. Fill the taco shells with the chicken and top with a dollop of Philly, serving 2 per person with the mango rice.

tip For a change, use soft flour tortillas instead of tacos.

Per serving: energy 572kcal, protein 32.2g, carbohydrate 70.7g, fat 18.2g, equivalent as salt 1.3g

apricot and almond chicken

serves 4 / prep time 15 minutes / cook time 15–20 minutes

1 tsp olive oil
4 boneless, skinless chicken
   breasts, sliced
1 small onion, finely chopped
½ tsp turmeric
½ tsp ground cinnamon
100g Philadelphia Extra Light
275ml skimmed milk
150g ready-to-eat apricots, halved
50g sultanas
25g flaked almonds

HEAT the oil in a large saucepan and brown the chicken over a medium heat for about 5 minutes. Add the onion, turmeric and cinnamon. Continue cooking for 3–4 minutes until the chicken is cooked through.

STIR the Philly, milk, apricots, sultanas and almonds into the pan. Cook over a low heat for 8–10 minutes, stirring occasionally, until the Philly has melted and the sauce has thickened.

tip Plain or fruity couscous is the perfect accompaniment. To make fruity couscous, stir sprigs of fresh lemon thyme, dried cranberries, sultanas, orange zest and pistachio pieces into the prepared couscous.

Per serving: energy 388kcal, protein 50.4g, carbohydrate 28.5g, fat 8.8g, equivalent as salt 0.53g

philly and ginger chicken with lemon rice

serves 4 / prep time 5 minutes / cook time 20 minutes

2 tbsp vegetable oil
3cm piece of fresh root ginger,
    peeled and grated
2 garlic cloves, crushed
3 fresh green chillies, deseeded
    and finely diced
4 boneless, skinless chicken
    breasts, cut into strips
120g Philadelphia Garlic & Herbs
200g basmati rice
3 cardamom pods
1 lemon

HEAT half the oil in a large saucepan, add the ginger, garlic and chillies and cook gently for 1 minute. Add the chicken and cook for 3–4 minutes. Stir in the Philly, adding a little water to make a sauce, then simmer for 5 minutes.

COOK the rice according to the packet instructions. In a large frying pan, heat the remaining oil, bruise the cardamom pods with a knife and add them to the pan. Using a vegetable peeler, shave off strips of the lemon peel and add to the pan, cooking for 2 minutes so they release their flavour and aroma.

TIP the cooked rice into the frying pan and stir well, coating it with the oil. Divide the rice among 4 plates and top with the chicken and a squeeze of lemon juice.

Per serving: energy 520kcal, protein 39.6g, carbohydrate 62.5g, fat 12.2g, equivalent as salt 0.8g

chicken, porcini and sweet marsala sauce

serves 2 / prep time 10 minutes / cook time 40 minutes

a drizzle of olive oil
1 large sprig of rosemary
2 red onions, sliced
2 garlic cloves, thinly sliced
2 boneless chicken breasts, skin on
25g dried porcini mushrooms
150ml sweet Marsala
100g Philadelphia Light
juice of 1 lemon
cooked pasta and seasonal
    vegetables, to serve

HEAT the oil in a large saucepan with the rosemary. Add the onions, then the garlic. Cook on a medium heat until softened, then remove from the pan and set aside. Add the chicken to the pan and brown on both sides.

MEANWHILE, place the porcini mushrooms and the Marsala in a covered dish and heat for 1 minute in the microwave (or warm through together in a small pan), until the mushrooms have softened and absorbed some of the Marsala.

ONCE the chicken is browned, return the onions and garlic to the pan with the mushrooms and Marsala. Cover the pan and gently simmer for about 30 minutes until the chicken is cooked. (Turn the chicken once during cooking so that both sides cook in the juices.)

REMOVE the chicken and keep warm. Stir the Philly into the pan and stir into the juices with the lemon juice. Season to taste and warm through until the sauce has a pourable consistency. Serve the warm chicken and sauce on a bed of pasta with seasonal vegetables.

tip Chicken thighs can be used instead of breasts, which also makes it a cheaper dish.

Per serving: energy 710kcal, protein 58.2g, carbohydrate 62.8g, fat 17.6g, equivalent as salt 1.0g

stir-fried chicken tortillas

serves 4 / prep time 15 minutes / cook time 15 minutes

1 tsp olive or sunflower oil
4 boneless, skinless chicken
    breasts, sliced
1 onion, thinly sliced
1 red pepper, thinly sliced
4 soft flour tortillas
120g Philadelphia Extra Light
2 tbsp skimmed milk
½ tsp paprika
pinch of cayenne pepper
1 small bag mixed lettuce leaves
12 cherry tomatoes, halved

PREHEAT the oven to 190°C, gas 5. Heat the oil in a large non-stick frying pan. Add the chicken and brown over a medium heat for approximately 5 minutes. Add the onion and pepper, cook for a further 5 minutes or until cooked through.

WARM the tortillas according to the packet instructions, then drape each tortilla over up-turned ramekins or ovenproof teacups on a baking sheet. Heat the tortillas in the oven for 5–8 minutes until they have become crisp. Remove from the oven and leave to cool, then remove from the ramekins or cups.

WHISK together the Philly, milk, paprika and cayenne and add to the chicken mixture. Continue cooking for 2 minutes to heat through. Place the lettuce and tomatoes in the bottom of each tortilla cup and top with the chicken mixture. Serve immediately.

tip Strips of turkey breast can be used in this recipe, as turkey is a lower-fat alternative to chicken.

Per serving: energy 459kcal, protein 61.8g, carbohydrate 42.1g, fat 5.9g, equivalent as salt 1.1g

chicken biryani

serves 4 / prep time 5–10 minutes / cook time 20–25 minutes

1 tbsp olive or sunflower oil
1 onion, finely chopped
2 boneless, skinless chicken
    breasts, diced
1 courgette, diced
1 tbsp curry powder or paste
225g easy-cook rice
550ml hot chicken stock
120g Philadelphia Light
25g flaked almonds, toasted

HEAT the oil in a deep saucepan and fry the onion on a medium heat until beginning to brown. Add the chicken to the pan and brown on all sides.

ADD the courgette and curry powder or paste and fry for 1 minute, then add the rice and stir well.

POUR in the stock and add the Philly. Stir, put the lid on and reduce the heat to low. Cook for 15 minutes or until the rice is cooked through, stirring once or twice during cooking. Add a little more liquid if it becomes too dry. Serve with the almonds sprinkled on top.

tip Adjust the heat level of the dish by choosing a curry powder or paste to suit your taste.

Per serving: energy 467kcal, protein 29.0g, carbohydrate 55.7g, fat 15.7g, equivalent as salt 1.4g

roast aubergine and chicken curry

serves 4 / prep time 10 minutes / cook time 20 minutes

1 aubergine
2 tbsp vegetable oil
1 onion, finely chopped
2 tbsp mild curry powder
8 boneless, skinless chicken
    thighs, cut into pieces
300ml chicken stock
120g Philadelphia Garlic & Herbs
roughly chopped fresh coriander,
    to garnish
cooked basmati rice and spinach,
    to serve

PREHEAT the oven to 190°C, gas mark 5. Place the whole aubergine directly onto the oven shelf and roast for 15 minutes. Remove and allow to cool slightly.

MEANWHILE, heat the oil in a medium saucepan and sauté the onion for 3–4 minutes until starting to soften. Sprinkle in the curry powder and cook for 1–2 minutes over a gentle heat, then add the chicken pieces and cook for 5 minutes, stirring occasionally. Add the stock and bring to the boil, then reduce the heat. Leave to simmer for about 15 minutes.

REMOVE the stalk from the aubergine, roughly dice the flesh and tip into the curry. Simmer for another 5 minutes. Stir in the Philly and warm through. Divide among 4 bowls and scatter with coriander. Serve with the rice with a good handful of spinach stirred through it.

Per serving: energy 589kcal, protein 33.4g, carbohydrate 56.7g, fat 25.2g, equivalent as salt 1.8g

chicken and nectarine salad

serves 4 / prep time 10 minutes / cook time 10 minutes

2 boneless, skinless chicken
    breasts, each approx. 150g
2 ripe nectarines, halved and
    stone removed
120g Philadelphia Light
2 tbsp sweet chilli sauce
1 tbsp chopped fresh coriander
2 tbsp milk
225g crisp lettuce leaves, such as
    Little Gem

COOK the chicken breasts in a griddle pan over a moderate heat for 4–5 minutes each side until cooked through (test with a skewer, the juices should run clear). About 2–3 minutes towards the end of the cooking time, add the nectarine halves and griddle on both sides.

MIX the Philly with the sweet chilli sauce, coriander and milk. Arrange the salad leaves on 4 plates, slice the chicken breasts and nectarines and divide among the plates. Serve with the Philly dressing.

Per serving: energy 184kcal, protein 22.3g, carbohydrate 13.5g, fat 4.8g, equivalent as salt 0.8g

chinese chicken salad

8 mini chicken fillets or
    chicken goujons
2 tsp five spice powder
100g Philadelphia Light
50g sesame seeds

For the salad and dressing:
2 oranges
50g rocket
100g beansprouts
1 tbsp olive oil
1 tbsp light soy sauce

PREHEAT the grill to Medium. Cut the mini fillets in half lengthways to give 16 pieces and rub with five spice powder. Spread the Philly over the chicken and roll it in the sesame seeds. Grill the chicken for 10–12 minutes until cooked through and lightly browned, turning occasionally.

PREPARE the salad. Using a sharp knife, remove the peel and pith of the oranges, over a bowl to catch any juice, and divide into segments. Keep the juice for the dressing.

PLACE the rocket, beansprouts and orange segments on 4 plates and top with the cooked chicken. Mix together 2 tablespoons of the reserved orange juice, the oil and soy sauce and spoon over. Serve immediately.

tip Alternatively, use chicken breasts and slice them yourself to make strips of chicken.

Per serving: energy 332kcal, protein 38.9g, carbohydrate 10.2g, fat 15.5g, equivalent as salt 1.0g

pork and mushroom stroganoff / sweet chilli pork kebabs / philly pork one-pot / rose veal with philly and mustard sauce / philly pork loin rolls with apricots / pork with philly, grain mustard and cider sauce / moussaka with creamy philly sauce / philly-stuffed shoulder of lamb / butterflied leg of lamb marinated in herbs and philly / lamb cutlets with cannellini beans, philly and rosemary / spiced lamb with philly and almonds / sirloin steak with basil and philly sauce / goulash with herby philly dumplings / chilli con carne / japanese seared beef with philly wasabi mash

MEAT

pork and mushroom stroganoff

serves 4 / prep time 10 minutes / cook time 20–25 minutes

225g brown rice
2 tbsp olive or sunflower oil
450g pork tenderloin fillet, sliced
     into strips
1 red onion, chopped
225g chestnut mushrooms, sliced
1 tbsp fresh sage, chopped
2 tbsp white wine
1 tsp wholegrain mustard
120g Philadelphia Light

COOK the rice according to the packet instructions. While the rice is cooking, prepare the stroganoff.

HEAT the oil in a large, deep frying pan and fry the pork in 2 batches over a high heat, browning on all sides. Lower the heat and fry the pork until cooked through. Remove the meat from the pan and set aside.

FRY the onion, mushrooms and sage for 2–3 minutes until beginning to brown.

STIR in the wine, mustard and Philly and stir well until all of the Philly has been incorporated. Return the pork to the pan, heat through, season with black pepper and serve with the rice.

tip As an alternative, use a mixture of wild and long grain rice instead of brown rice.

Per serving: energy 536kcal, protein 43.4g, carbohydrate 50.8g, fat 18.4g, equivalent as salt 0.6g

sweet chilli pork kebabs

serves 4 / prep time 10 minutes, plus 30 minutes marinating / cook time 7–8 minutes

100g Philadelphia Extra Light
1 tbsp soy sauce
3 tbsp sweet chilli sauce
1 tbsp chopped fresh coriander
450g lean pork loin, cut into
    2.5cm cubes
2 corn on the cob, cut into pieces
120g mixed salad leaves, to serve

COMBINE the Philly, soy sauce, chilli sauce and coriander in a bowl. Add the pork cubes and marinate for 20–30 minutes, or ideally overnight.

THREAD the pork onto 4 large or 8 small skewers (if using wooden skewers, soak them in water for 30 minutes first to avoid them burning). Grill on the barbecue for 7–8 minutes, turning occasionally, until browned and cooked through.

SERVE with barbecued corn on the cob and a good handful of salad leaves.

tip Take care not to overcook the pork, as it is so lean it will dry out if cooked for too long.

Per serving: energy 182kcal, protein 27.5g, carbohydrate 4.9g, fat 5.8g, equivalent as salt 2.3g

philly pork one-pot

serves 4 / prep time 5 minutes / cook time 40 minutes

1 tbsp vegetable oil
3 onions, finely sliced
600g pork shoulder chops,
    cut into chunks
25g fresh sage, leaves chopped
400ml vegetable stock
120g Philadelphia Chives
500g new potatoes
green vegetable, to serve

HEAT the oil in a large saucepan with a lid, add the onions and cook over a medium heat for 10 minutes, stirring regularly, until they start to brown. Turn up the heat, add the pork and brown it on all sides. Sprinkle in the sage, stir, then add the stock and bring to a simmer. Put the lid on and cook for 30 minutes until the pork is tender and cooked through. Stir in the Philly and season to taste.

MEANWHILE, cook the potatoes in a pan of boiling water for 15–20 minutes until they are cooked through, then drain and crush them slightly and season to taste. Serve the potatoes accompanied by a good spoonful of Philly one-pot and your favourite green vegetable.

Per serving: energy 659kcal, protein 35.7g, carbohydrate 33.8g, fat 43.1g, equivalent as salt 1.3g

rose veal with philly and mustard sauce

serves 2 / prep time 5 minutes / cook time 15 minutes

1 tbsp olive oil
4 rose veal escalopes
100ml vegetable stock
60g Philadelphia
1 tbsp white wine vinegar
25g fresh dill, chopped
200g green beans, to serve

IN a large frying pan, heat the oil until quite hot then fry the veal for 1½ minutes on each side until golden brown. Remove from the pan and set aside on a warm plate to rest.

USING kitchen paper, wipe any excess oil from the pan then pour in the stock, Philly and vinegar. Stir well and simmer until thickened. Stir in the dill.

COOK the green beans in boiling water for 10 minutes until just soft. Serve with the veal and pour over the sauce.

tip The sauce also works well with chicken.

Per serving: energy 428kcal, protein 59.2g, carbohydrate 3.4g, fat 19.7g, equivalent as salt 0.8g

philly pork loin rolls with apricots

serves 4 / prep time 15 minutes / cook time 15 minutes

200g Philadelphia Light
175g finely chopped dried apricots
1 tbsp chopped fresh tarragon
4 pork loin steaks, each approx. 125g
a drizzle of olive oil
300g fine egg noodles
2 tbsp light soy sauce
1 tsp grated fresh root ginger
3 spring onions, chopped
1 tbsp chopped fresh flatleaf parsley

PREHEAT the oven to 200°C, gas 6. Mix the Philly, apricots and tarragon in a bowl. Season with salt and black pepper.

TRIM any fat from the pork loins, then place each one in turn on a chopping board, cover it with a layer of cling film and flatten out using a rolling pin. Spread each loin with the Philly stuffing, roll up individually and tie using string. Heat the oil in an ovenproof frying pan and cook the pork rolls over a medium heat for about 5 minutes until browned. Transfer the pan to the oven and continue cooking for 10 minutes.

WHILE the pork is cooking, prepare the egg noodles following the packet instructions. Drain, then toss with the soy sauce, ginger, spring onions and parsley. Remove the pork from the oven, take off the string and cut the rolls into slices. Serve on a bed of warm noodles.

Per serving: energy 592kcal, protein 42.2g, carbohydrate 60.1g, fat 21.8g, equivalent as salt 1.0g

pork with philly, grain mustard and cider sauce

serves 4 / prep time 5 minutes / cook time 10 minutes

4 lean pork loin chops
100g Philadelphia Light
2 tsp wholegrain mustard
3 tbsp cider
200g broccoli, cut into florets
200g carrots, sliced
600g new potatoes

GRILL or barbecue the pork until cooked through (for about 8–10 minutes, depending on the thickness).

IN a small saucepan, gently heat together the Philly, mustard and cider but do not allow the sauce to boil.

MICROWAVE or steam the broccoli and carrots until tender and boil the new potatoes in a saucepan of lightly salted water until cooked. Serve the pork chops with the Philly sauce and the vegetables.

Per serving: energy 389kcal, protein 31.7g, carbohydrate 13.0g, fat 25.8g, equivalent as salt 1.0g

moussaka with creamy philly sauce

serves 4 / prep time 15 minutes / cook time 30 minutes

1 egg
120g Philadelphia Garlic & Herbs
150g 0% fat Greek yoghurt
40g Parmesan, finely grated
400g lean minced lamb
1 aubergine, sliced lengthways
1 onion, diced
2 x 400g cans chopped tomatoes
1 cinnamon stick (optional)

PREHEAT the oven to 190°C, gas 5. Beat the egg in a bowl with the Philly, yoghurt and half the Parmesan.

IN a frying pan, brown the mince over a high heat. When cooked, remove with a slotted spoon, leaving behind the lamb fat. In the same pan set over a medium heat, fry the aubergine slices until brown on both sides, set aside on kitchen paper and season to taste. Add the onion to the pan and fry gently (add a little oil if necessary). Once softened, return the meat to the pan, stir in the chopped tomatoes and add the cinnamon, if using. Simmer for 10 minutes then season to taste.

REMOVE the cinnamon stick, if using, then pour half the mince into an ovenproof dish, top with half the aubergine slices and repeat. Top with the Philly mixture then sprinkle with the remaining Parmesan. Cook for 30 minutes until browned.

tip If the mince mixture gets a little dry, add a slosh of red wine or beef stock.

Per serving: energy 337kcal, protein 31.0g, carbohydrate 30.3g, fat 10.5g, equivalent as salt 0.5g

philly-stuffed shoulder of lamb

serves 6 / prep time 10 minutes / cook time 1 hour 20 minutes

1 small bunch of fresh sage, reserve
    2 sprigs to garnish
180g Philadelphia Garlic & Herbs
1 lamb shoulder, off the bone, excess
    fat removed
1 tbsp olive oil
200ml vegetable stock
new potatoes and green vegetables,
    to serve

PREHEAT the oven to 180°C, gas 4. Finely dice the sage and mix it with the Philly.

FLATTEN out the lamb using a rolling pin, spread the Philly down the centre then roll the lamb back up and tie it securely with string. Place the lamb in a large casserole dish with a lid, drizzle with oil and pour the stock around it. Put on the lid and roast for 1 hour.

REMOVE the lid and cook for a further 20 minutes until the meat has browned. Take out of the oven and garnish with the reserved sage sprigs. Serve with new potatoes and green vegetables.

Per serving: energy 324kcal, protein 21.1g, carbohydrate 1.3g, fat 26.1g, equivalent as salt 0.7g

butterflied leg of lamb marinated in herbs and philly

serves 4 / prep time 10 minutes, plus overnight marinating / cook time 20–30 minutes

juice of 1 lemon
3 garlic cloves, crushed
120g Philadelphia Basil
2 tbsp olive oil
8 sprigs of fresh rosemary, finely chopped
½ leg lamb, boned and butterflied to 4cm thick
green salad, to serve

COMBINE everything except the lamb in a large bowl or container with a lid. Add the lamb and rub in the marinade, working it into the meat. Leave to marinate overnight, or for as long as possible.

WHEN ready to cook, preheat the oven to 180°C, gas 4. Heat an ovenproof frying pan or skillet until quite hot and sear the lamb on all sides, browning well all over. Transfer to the oven and cook for 20–30 minutes, depending on how well you like it done.

SERVE cut into thick slices with a green salad on the side.

tip You could substitute the Philadelphia Basil for Philadelphia Chives, if you prefer.

Per serving: energy 481kcal, protein 41.2g, carbohydrate 3.4g, fat 33.6g, equivalent as salt 0.3g

lamb cutlets with cannellini beans, philly and rosemary

serves 4 / prep time 10 minutes / cook time 15 minutes

2 x 400g cans cannellini beans
100g Philadelphia Garlic & Herbs
100ml vegetable stock
8 sprigs of fresh rosemary
12 lamb chops, well trimmed of fat
extra virgin olive oil
1 lemon, cut into 4 wedges, to serve

PREHEAT the grill to High. Drain the beans and rinse well. Combine the Philly, stock and half the rosemary sprigs in a saucepan and heat gently. Add the drained beans and simmer, stirring occasionally, for 10 minutes. Season to taste.

BRUSH the lamb chops with a little oil and cook quickly under the hot grill until well-browned but still a little pink inside.

MASH the bean mixture slightly with a fork so it retains a chunky texture then divide it among 4 plates. Arrange 3 lamb chops on each pile of beans, tuck in the remaining rosemary sprigs, and serve with lemon wedges.

Per serving: energy 695kcal, protein 77.8g, carbohydrate 27.4g, fat 30.5g, equivalent as salt 0.8g

spiced lamb with philly and almonds

serves 4 / prep time 5 minutes / cook time 35 minutes

120g Philadelphia
100g ground almonds
4cm piece of fresh root ginger,
    peeled and chopped
2 garlic cloves
1 tsp garam masala
1 tbsp olive oil
1kg lamb pieces
1 onion, thinly sliced
flat breads and salad, to serve

PLACE the Philly, almonds, ginger and garlic in a blender with 200ml water and blend until smooth. Stir in the garam masala.

HEAT the oil in a large saucepan, brown the lamb on all sides over a medium heat then remove from the pan. Lower the heat, tip in the onion and cook until it is soft and brown. Return the meat to the pan and pour over the sauce. Bring to a simmer and put a lid on the pan. Cook for 30 minutes until the lamb is cooked and tender.

SERVE with flat breads and salad.

Per serving: energy 643kcal, protein 57.8g, carbohydrate 6.7g, fat 42.9g, equivalent as salt 0.3g

sirloin steak with basil and philly sauce

serves 2 / prep time 10 minutes / cook time 25 minutes

2 beef sirloin steaks
1 tsp olive oil
300g pappardelle or linguine
2 shallots, finely chopped
100ml dry white wine (or stock if you prefer)
2 tomatoes, skinned, deseeded and chopped
60g Philadelphia Garlic & Herbs
6 sprigs of fresh basil

TRIM any visible fat from the steaks then season both sides with black pepper. Heat the oil in a frying pan over a moderate heat and fry the steaks for 4–5 minutes for rare, 8–10 minutes for medium and 10–12 minutes for well done, turning once during cooking. Remove from the pan and set aside.

COOK the pasta according to the packet instructions.

ADD the shallots to the meat pan and cook for 2–3 minutes until softened, then pour in the wine (or stock), bring to the boil and reduce by half. Stir in the tomatoes and Philly and simmer for 1–2 minutes while you shred the basil.

REDUCE the heat and stir in the basil. Season to taste. Divide the pasta among 2 plates and top with the steak and sauce.

Per serving: energy 962kcal, protein 75.1g, carbohydrate 114.5g, fat 19.2g, equivalent as salt 1.0g

goulash with herby philly dumplings

serves 4 / prep time 10 minutes / cook time 50 minutes

1 tbsp olive oil
500g sirloin steak, trimmed and
    cut into chunks
1 onion, peeled and thinly sliced
150g self-raising flour
3 tbsp paprika
3 tbsp tomato purée
450ml beef stock
100g Philadelphia Garlic & Herbs

PREHEAT the oven to 180°C, gas 4. In a casserole dish with a lid, heat the oil, brown the steak on all sides, then remove with a slotted spoon. Do this in 2 batches if necessary. Turn the heat down to medium, tip in the onion, stir, then put the lid on and cook for 5 minutes until it browns and softens.

RETURN the beef to the pan, sprinkle over a tablespoon of the flour, the paprika and the tomato purée, stir in for 1 minute then slowly pour in the stock, bit by bit, stirring as you go. Put the lid on and pop into the oven for 20 minutes.

WHILE the beef is cooking, mix the remaining flour with the Philly, add 5 teaspoons of water to make a dough and form into 8 balls. Once the goulash has cooked for 20 minutes, take off the lid and add the dumplings. Cook for a further 20 minutes or until the meat is tender.

tip If you want to sneak in some extra veg, add some diced red and green pepper when you're browning the onion.

Per serving: 427kcal, protein 37.8g, carbohydrate 40.1g, fat 14.1g, equivalent as salt 2.0g

chilli con carne

serves 6 / prep time 25 minutes / cook time 45 minutes

400g lean minced beef
1 medium onion, finely diced
1 garlic clove, finely chopped
2 tsp chilli powder (mild or hot)
100g tomato salsa (mild or hot)
1 red pepper, diced
400g can chopped tomatoes
400g can kidney beans in water,
    drained and rinsed
6 soft flour tortillas
120g Philadelphia Light
1 small ripe avocado, halved,
    stoned, peeled and thickly sliced
2 tomatoes, diced
fresh coriander, to garnish

COOK the minced beef in a large non-stick saucepan over a medium heat, stirring occasionally. Add the onion and garlic and cook until softened. Stir in the chilli powder, cook a further minute, then add the salsa, pepper, chopped tomatoes and kidney beans. Simmer for 30–35 minutes until heated through.

MEANWHILE, warm the tortillas according to the packet instructions. Drape each tortilla over an upturned ovenproof teacup or ramekin. Place on a baking sheet and cook for 5–8 minutes at 190°C, gas 5 until lightly golden. Leave to cool slightly, then carefully remove the tortillas.

PLACE a little cooked chilli into each tortilla cup and top with a spoonful of Philly (softened with a little milk, if desired), slices of avocado, diced tomatoes and a little coriander.

tip If you do not have a non-stick saucepan, dab a little oil onto kitchen paper and wipe around the inside of the pan before using.

Per serving: energy 398kcal, protein 25.1g, carbohydrate 47.7g, fat 13.6g, equivalent as salt 1.3g

creamy lemon and thyme spaghetti / spinach and philly lasagne / asparagus, philly and mint tagliatelle / philly and cauliflower pasta bake / creamy mushroom pappardelle / creamy sweet potato and blue cheese gnocchi / mixed pepper and herb cannelloni / spaghetti with sun-dried tomatoes and capers / linguine with philly, lobster and garlic / smoked salmon pasta / thai-spiced prawns with tagliatelle / chicken and sunblush tomato pasta / chicken and olive penne / pasta shells stuffed with bacon, philly and pine nuts / creamy mushroom and bacon gnocchi / philly, tomato and pesto pasta / ham and leek cannelloni / white ragù with rigatoni / spaghetti carbonara / bacon and tomato lasagne / creamy mushroom risotto / courgette risotto with philly, olives and feta / philly risotto with butternut squash and sage / smoked salmon, chive, philly and lemon risotto / herb risotto / smoked haddock and leek risotto / asparagus and smoked ham risotto

PASTA AND RISOTTO

spinach and philly lasagne

serves 6 / prep time 20 minutes / cook time 30 minutes

1 tbsp olive oil
1 onion, chopped
1 garlic clove, crushed
2 celery sticks, finely chopped
2 carrots, finely chopped
1 tbsp tomato purée
800g can chopped tomatoes
pinch of sugar (optional)
1kg frozen spinach
300g Philadelphia Light
3 tbsp grated Parmesan
2 tbsp fresh mint leaves, chopped
10 no-cook lasagne sheets
salad and crusty bread, to serve

FIRST make the tomato sauce; heat the oil in a large saucepan set over a low heat and soften the onion, garlic, celery and carrots – try not to let them colour. Stir in the tomato purée and continue cooking for another 5 minutes before adding the tomatoes. Simmer for about 20 minutes. Using a liquidiser or hand-held blender, purée the sauce until smooth – it should be thick. Add a pinch of sugar if the tomatoes taste acidic.

WHILE the sauce is cooking, make the spinach filling. Put the frozen spinach into a pan and heat gently until it has defrosted. Drain any additional liquid. Set aside to cool.

PREHEAT the oven to 180°C, gas 4. Put the Philly in a separate bowl and stir until smooth, then add the spinach, half the Parmesan and the mint. Spread a thin layer of tomato sauce in an ovenproof dish, followed by a layer of the spinach mixture and top with some lasagne sheets. Repeat, ending with a layer of tomato sauce.

SPRINKLE the top with the remaining Parmesan and bake the lasagne for about 30 minutes until bubbling and golden on top. Serve with salad and crusty bread.

tip For extra texture, add in 30g pine nuts with the Philly.

Per serving: energy 336kcal, protein 18.1g, carbohydrate 39.9g, fat 11.5g, equivalent as salt 0.7g

asparagus, philly and mint tagliatelle

serves 4 / prep time 5 minutes / cook time 15 minutes

1 bunch of asparagus, woody
    ends cut off
2 tsp olive oil
1 onion, finely chopped
120g Philadelphia Garlic & Herbs
350g tagliatelle
small bunch of fresh mint, leaves
    chopped

CUT the tips off the asparagus and set aside, then chop the stalks into discs less than 1cm thick. Heat the oil in a saucepan, add the onion and fry gently until soft and golden. Add the asparagus stalks and tips and cook for a minute. Stir in the Philly and season well with black pepper.

COOK the tagliatelle according to the packet instructions. Use a little of the pasta water to loosen the sauce if it's too thick, and when cooked drain the tagliatelle and add it to the saucepan, stirring well to coat.

SPRINKLE over the mint, stir a final time, then divide among 4 pasta bowls.

Per serving: energy 385kcal, protein 13.8g, carbohydrate 69.3g, fat 7.9g, equivalent as salt 0.3g

philly and cauliflower pasta bake

serves 6 / prep time 20 minutes / cook time 20 minutes

300g penne
1 medium cauliflower
300ml milk
180g Philadelphia Garlic & Herbs
1 tsp freshly grated nutmeg (optional)
butter for greasing

PREHEAT the oven to 200°C, gas 6. Cook the penne according to the packet instructions, then drain.

MEANWHILE, divide the cauliflower into small florets and cook in a saucepan of boiling water for 10 minutes until it is al dente. In a separate pan, heat the milk and whisk in the Philly and nutmeg, then simmer until it reaches a thicker saucy consistency. Season to taste.

GREASE the inside of an ovenproof dish with the butter and tip in the penne and cauliflower, distributing them both evenly around the dish. Pour over the sauce and bake in the oven for 20 minutes until the top is nicely browned.

Per serving: energy 290kcal, protein 13.1g, carbohydrate 42.4g, fat 8.0g, equivalent as salt 0.5g

creamy mushroom pappardelle

serves 2 / prep time 10 minutes / cook time 15 minutes

200g pappardelle (or tagliatelle)
10g unsalted butter
1 garlic clove, finely chopped
a few sprigs of fresh thyme, woody
    stems removed
250g mushrooms (try a selection
    of button, brown cap, Portobello),
    wiped and sliced
60g Philadelphia Light
30g grated Parmesan
15g fresh flatleaf parsley, roughly
    chopped

COOK the pasta for 12–15 minutes in a saucepan of boiling water or according to the packet instructions.

MEANWHILE, gently melt the butter in a large pan, add the garlic and thyme and cook over a medium heat for 1 minute. Add the mushrooms and cook until the juices are running. Stir in the Philly and warm over a low heat until it melts. Sprinkle over half the Parmesan and parsley and some black pepper to taste. Stir until smooth.

KEEP warm over a low heat until the pasta is cooked. Drain the pasta and add to the sauce. Mix well, until coated. Top with the remaining Parmesan and parsley.

tip Delicious with rocket leaves or French beans.

Per serving: energy 526kcal, protein 23.2g, carbohydrate 76.9g, fat 15.5g, equivalent as salt 0.7g

creamy sweet potato and blue cheese gnocchi

serves 4 / prep time 15 minutes / cook time 20 minutes

500g gnocchi
1 sweet potato (about 200g), peeled and cut into small chunks
2 tsp olive oil
150g flat mushrooms, wiped and sliced
75g Philadelphia Light, softened
3 tbsp milk
50g Danish Blue cheese, crumbled
2 tbsp chopped fresh chives
mixed salad, to serve (optional)

COOK the gnocchi and sweet potato in a large saucepan of boiling water for 5 minutes or until the gnocchi floats to the surface. Drain.

MEANWHILE, heat the oil in a frying pan and cook the mushrooms over a medium heat until browned. Add the Philly and milk to the pan and gently simmer, stirring occasionally, until the sauce is smooth and has heated through.

ADD the Danish Blue, gnocchi and sweet potato to the mushroom mixture. Toss to coat, and continue cooking over a low heat until the gnocchi is heated through. Top with fresh chives and serve with a mixed salad, if liked.

Per serving: energy 375kcal, protein 12.0g, carbohydrate 61.8g, fat 8.9g, equivalent as salt 2.3g

mixed pepper and herb cannelloni

serves 2 / prep time 20 minutes / cook time 15–20 minutes

1 tbsp olive or sunflower oil,
    plus extra for greasing
1 onion, finely chopped
½ red pepper, thinly sliced
½ yellow pepper, thinly sliced
60g Philadelphia Garlic & Herbs
1 tbsp milk
2 large sheets fresh lasagne
400g can chopped tomatoes,
    drained
1 tsp dried mixed herbs
large handful of rocket, to serve

PREHEAT the oven to 190°C, gas 5. Heat the oil in a frying pan and fry the onion and peppers over a medium heat for 3–4 minutes until softened and beginning to brown. Off the heat, stir in the Philly and milk.

FOLLOW the packet instructions for cooking the lasagne (it may be necessary to soak it in boiling water for 5 minutes to soften). Cut each sheet in half widthways. In a small pan, heat the tomatoes with the herbs.

PLACE a spoonful of the Philly and pepper mixture at one end of each piece of lasagne and roll up into a tube. Place all 4 into a greased ovenproof dish. Pour over the tomato mixture and bake for 15–20 minutes. Serve with the rocket leaves.

tip For a quick alternative, drain a can of chopped tomatoes with herbs and tip the tomatoes straight over the filled pasta tubes before baking.

Per serving: energy 350kcal, protein 12.0g, carbohydrate 52.2g, fat 11.8g, equivalent as salt 0.6g

spaghetti with sun-dried tomatoes and capers

serves 6 / prep time 10 minutes / cook time 15 minutes

750g spaghetti
a drizzle of olive oil
1 red onion, finely diced
2 tomatoes, skinned, deseeded
    and diced
180g Philadelphia
6 sun-dried tomatoes, chopped
1 tbsp capers
6 anchovy fillets, chopped
fresh basil leaves, to garnish

COOK the pasta according to the packet instructions.

MEANWHILE, in a large frying pan, heat the oil and gently cook the onion for 2–3 minutes until soft. Add the tomatoes and cook for 1 minute, stir in the Philly then the sun-dried tomatoes, capers and anchovies and heat through.

ONCE the spaghetti is cooked, drain and add it to the sauce, tossing well to coat thoroughly. Divide among 6 plates and scatter with basil leaves.

Per serving: energy 573kcal, protein 18.5g, carbohydrate 97.1g, fat 15.0g, equivalent as salt 1.3g

linguine with philly, lobster and garlic

serves 6 / prep time 10 minutes / cook time 15 minutes

600g linguine
1 tsp olive oil
1 garlic clove, diced
180g Philadelphia Garlic & Herbs
juice of 1 lemon
2 cooked lobster tails
12 cooked, peeled prawns
4 sprigs of fresh lemon thyme,
    leaves picked off

COOK the pasta according to the packet instructions.

MEANWHILE, heat the oil in a frying pan, add the garlic and cook gently so as not to burn it. Add the Philly and lemon juice and a few spoonfuls of the pasta water to make a smooth sauce.

CUT the lobster tails into medallions and add them to the sauce along with the prawns and thyme leaves. Cook on a gentle heat for 4–5 minutes until they are heated through. Season to taste.

DIVIDE the pasta among 6 plates and top with the sauce.

tip If you can't find lobster tails, use big, cooked and peeled tiger prawns instead.

Per serving: energy 451kcal, protein 21.7g, carbohydrate 74.5g, fat 7.4g, equivalent as salt 1.0g

smoked salmon pasta

serves 4 / prep time 5 minutes / cook time 15 minutes

250g tagliatelle
200g Philadelphia Light
2 tbsp milk
juice of ½ lemon
125g smoked salmon, thinly sliced
200g sugar snap peas, cooked

COOK the pasta according to the packet instructions.

MEANWHILE, spoon the Philly into a small saucepan with the milk and lemon juice. Stir over a gentle heat until the Philly has melted.

DRAIN the pasta and add to the sauce. Stir together until the Philly has coated all the pasta. Gently mix in the smoked salmon, sugar snap peas and season with black pepper.

Per serving: energy 339kcal, protein 22.0g, carbohydrate 39.5g, fat 11.3g, equivalent as salt 2.0g

thai-spiced prawns with tagliatelle

serves 4 / prep time 5 minutes / cook time 20 minutes

300g tagliatelle
1 tbsp olive oil
350g cooked tiger prawns
   (frozen or chilled)
2 tbsp red Thai curry paste
2 tbsp dry white wine
400g can chopped tomatoes
100g Philadelphia Light
handful of chopped fresh
   coriander leaves

COOK the tagliatelle according to the packet instructions.

MEANWHILE, heat the oil in a medium saucepan, add the prawns and cook for 3–4 minutes.

ADD the Thai curry paste, wine and tomatoes and cook for a further 3–4 minutes, stir in the Philly and the coriander and heat through.

DRAIN the pasta and serve with the prawn sauce.

tips If using frozen prawns, defrost before use. The sauce would also work well with noodles or rice instead of pasta.

To reduce the salt content, replace the prawns with cooked chicken or a selection of vegetables and use a little less curry paste.

Per serving: energy 427kcal, protein 25.8g, carbohydrate 60.0g, fat 10.0g, equivalent as salt 2.0g

chicken and sunblush tomato pasta

serves 4 / prep time 5 minutes / cook time 15–20 minutes

300g pasta shapes (e.g. spirals, penne or shells)
1 tbsp olive oil
2 boneless, skinless chicken breasts, cut into strips
120g Philadelphia Garlic & Herbs
1 tbsp milk
2 tsp sun-dried tomato paste
50g SunBlush tomatoes, chopped
1 tbsp chopped fresh flatleaf parsley

COOK the pasta according to the packet instructions. Drain.

HEAT the oil in a griddle pan and cook the chicken over a medium heat for about 5–8 minutes until browned and cooked through.

HEAT the Philly gently in a small saucepan with the milk, sun-dried tomato paste, SunBlush tomatoes and chopped parsley. Add the cooked chicken strips and heat through. Combine with the pasta and serve straight away.

tip If you don't have a griddle pan, simply cook the chicken in a frying pan with ½ tablespoon olive oil.

Per serving: energy 471kcal, protein 31.2g, carbohydrate 56.8g, fat 13.4g, equivalent as salt 0.5g

chicken and olive penne

serves 2 / prep time 10–12 minutes / cook time 10–15 minutes

1 tbsp olive oil
2 boneless, skinless chicken breasts,
    cut into pieces
½ sprig fresh rosemary, chopped
½ tbsp grated Parmesan
250g fresh penne
½ red pepper, finely diced
½ tbsp chopped fresh flatleaf parsley
100g Philadelphia Light
4–5 tbsp milk
1 tbsp black or green olives, pitted
    and sliced

HEAT half the oil in a large frying pan and fry the chicken until golden brown. Add the rosemary and Parmesan and season with black pepper. Continue cooking over a medium heat until the chicken is thoroughly cooked.

COOK the pasta according to the packet instructions. Drain.

IN a large saucepan, fry the red pepper gently in the remaining oil and add the parsley, Philly and milk. Stir until melted then add the drained pasta, olives and chicken.

tip Serve this tasty pasta dish with a basil and tomato salad for a simple midweek supper.

Per serving: energy 717kcal, protein 62.5g, carbohydrate 75.7g, fat 20.3g, equivalent as salt 1.8g

pasta shells stuffed with bacon, philly and pine nuts

serves 4 / prep time 15 minutes / cook time 20 minutes

100g pine nuts
1 tbsp olive oil
6 rashers smoked bacon, chopped
    into small pieces
120g Philadelphia Garlic & Herbs
300g giant pasta shells
1 onion, diced
500g carton tomato passata
few shavings of Parmesan (optional)

PREHEAT the oven to 180°C, gas 4. In a frying pan, dry-fry the pine nuts over a medium heat until golden then transfer to a bowl and set aside. In the same pan, heat half of the oil, add the bacon pieces and cook, stirring occasionally, until browned. Tip into the bowl with the pine nuts, add the Philly and mix well.

COOK the pasta according to the packet instructions. Drain, then fill each shell with the Philly mix and place in the bottom of an ovenproof dish.

IN the same frying pan, heat the remaining oil, cook the onion for 5 minutes then add the passata. Cook for 5 minutes until reduced slightly, then pour over the pasta and bake for 20 minutes. Serve topped with a few shavings of Parmesan, if using.

Per serving: energy 612kcal, protein 23.5g, carbohydrate 65.8g, fat 28.5g, equivalent as salt 2.0g

creamy mushroom and bacon gnocchi

serves 4 / prep time 15 minutes / cook time 20 minutes

500g gnocchi
2 tsp olive oil
2–3 rashers bacon, trimmed of fat
    and cut into strips
150g flat mushrooms, sliced
1 red onion, cut into thin wedges
60g Philadelphia Light, softened
3 tbsp milk
2 garlic cloves, finely sliced
handful of fresh basil leaves, plus
    extra to garnish

COOK the gnocchi in a large saucepan of boiling water for 5 minutes, or until they float to the surface. Drain.

HEAT the oil in a frying pan and cook the bacon, mushrooms and onion over a medium heat until browned. Remove from the pan. Add the Philly, milk and garlic to the pan and gently simmer, stirring occasionally, until smooth and heated through.

RETURN the bacon mixture to the pan with the gnocchi. Toss to coat, and continue cooking over a low heat until the gnocchi is heated through. Stir in the basil leaves and serve immediately, garnished with extra basil leaves.

Per serving: energy 314kcal, protein 12.0g, carbohydrate 53.1g, fat 5.8g, equivalent as salt 2.3g

philly, tomato and pesto pasta

serves 2 / prep time 10 minutes / cook time 15 minutes

150g spiral-shaped pasta (e.g. fusilli)
1 tsp olive oil
150g chestnut mushrooms, sliced
2 tbsp green pesto
100g Philadelphia Light
200g cherry tomatoes, halved
a large handful of fresh basil leaves

COOK the pasta in a large saucepan of boiling water according to the packet instructions.

MEANWHILE, in a large pan, heat the oil and gently fry the mushrooms. Add the pesto and Philly and stir over a gentle heat until smooth.

ADD the drained pasta, tomatoes and basil leaves, stir to coat, and serve.

Per serving: energy 540kcal, protein 20.5g, carbohydrate 60.5g, fat 23.9g, equivalent as salt 0.3g

ham and leek cannelloni

serves 4 / prep time 20 minutes / cook time 20 minutes

3 leeks
300ml vegetable stock
120g Philadelphia Garlic & Herbs
85g smoked ham
12 cannelloni tubes
a drizzle of olive oil
1 onion, diced
400g can chopped tomatoes
40g pecorino cheese, grated
green salad, to serve

PREHEAT the oven to 180°C, gas 4. Slice the leeks thinly and, in a medium saucepan, simmer for 5 minutes in the stock. When they start to soften, lift them from the stock with a slotted spoon and reserve the stock.

IN a bowl, mix the leeks with the Philly and ham and season to taste. Stuff each cannelloni tube with some Philly mixture and lay side by side in an ovenproof dish.

HEAT a frying pan and sauté the onion over a medium heat in the oil. Add the tomatoes and the reserved stock and simmer for 10 minutes. Season to taste. Pour the tomatoes over the cannelloni tubes and top with the pecorino. Cook in the oven for 20 minutes until the pasta is soft and cooked through. Serve with a green salad.

Per serving: energy 405kcal, protein 21.5g, carbohydrate 56.5g, fat 10.7g, equivalent as salt 1.8g

white ragù with rigatoni

serves 4 / prep time 10 minutes / cook time 40 minutes

2 tbsp olive oil
1 onion, finely chopped
400g minced beef
400ml vegetable stock
120g Philadelphia Garlic & Herbs
500g rigatoni
60g freshly grated Parmesan

HEAT the oil in a large saucepan and gently fry the onion until softened and golden. Add the beef and mix well, allowing it to crumble. Cook for 10 minutes, stirring frequently, until the meat has browned. Pour off any fat then add the stock and simmer, uncovered, for 30 minutes, stirring occasionally. If it dries out too much, add a little more stock. Mix in the Philly and season to taste.

MEANWHILE, cook the pasta according to the packet instructions, drain, and add immediately to the sauce. Stir well, then divide among 4 plates and sprinkle over the Parmesan.

Per serving: energy 855kcal, protein 43.4g, carbohydrate 95.7g, fat 33.3g, equivalent as salt 1.8g

spaghetti carbonara

serves 4 : prep time 10 minutes / cook time 10 minutes

300g spaghetti
1 tbsp olive oil
1 small onion, finely sliced
1 garlic clove, crushed
120g Philadelphia Light, softened
75ml milk
4 slices smoked ham, diced
15g fresh flatleaf parsley, roughly
    chopped

COOK the spaghetti in a large saucepan of boiling water for about 8 minutes or according to the packet instructions.

HEAT the oil in a frying pan and gently cook the onion and garlic until softened. Add the Philly and milk and continue to cook over a low heat until the Philly has melted. Stir in the ham pieces.

DRAIN the pasta and return to the saucepan with the Philly mixture and all but 1 tablespoon of the chopped parsley. Gently stir the Philly mixture through the pasta and garnish with the remaining parsley.

tip As an alternative, use pieces of cooked crispy bacon or pancetta instead of the ham.

Per serving: energy 274kcal, protein 13.3g, carbohydrate 38.5g, fat 8.5g, equivalent as salt 1.0g

bacon and tomato lasagne

serves 4 / prep time 15–20 minutes / cook time 20–25 minutes

6 sheets fresh lasagne
1 tbsp olive or sunflower oil
1 red onion, chopped
6 rashers reduced-salt back
　　bacon, diced
6 medium tomatoes, skinned,
　　deseeded and chopped
1 tsp dried mixed herbs
60g Philadelphia Light
2 tbsp milk

For the topping:
60g Philadelphia Light
2 tbsp milk
25g Cheddar, grated
1 tsp Dijon mustard
mixed fresh chopped herbs,
　　to garnish

PREHEAT the oven to 190°C, gas 5. Follow the packet instructions to cook the lasagne (it may be necessary to soak the sheets in boiling water for 5 minutes to soften). Heat the oil in a medium saucepan and fry the onion and bacon over a medium heat for 3–4 minutes until beginning to brown.

ADD the tomatoes and herbs, reduce the heat to a simmer and cook for a further 3–4 minutes. Stir in the Philly and the milk off the heat.

PLACE 2 sheets of lasagne in an ovenproof dish, top with half the tomato mixture, then repeat with 2 more sheets of lasagne and the remaining tomato mixture. Finish with the remaining lasagne sheets. Mix together the topping ingredients and spread on top. Bake for 20 minutes or until browned. Serve sprinkled with fresh herbs.

tip To make 4 individual lasagnes, cut the lasagne sheets in half and divide the mixture among 4 individual-sized ovenproof dishes. Test the lasagnes with the point of a knife after 15 minutes of cooking as they may not need the full 20 minutes.

Per serving: energy 543kcal, protein 27.1g, carbohydrate 65.2g, fat 21.1g, equivalent as salt 2.0g

creamy mushroom risotto

serves 4 / prep time 10–12 minutes / cook time 30 minutes

2 tsp olive oil
200g risotto rice (Arborio or
    Carnaroli are best)
600ml hot vegetable stock
350g mixed mushrooms, cut into
    large pieces
1 garlic clove, crushed
120g Philadelphia Light
a little skimmed milk (optional)
a handful of fresh flatleaf parsley,
    roughly chopped

HEAT half the oil in a large saucepan. Add the rice and gently fry over a medium heat for 2 minutes or until lightly golden. Gradually add the stock and 300ml hot water then bring to the boil. Simmer for 20 minutes, stirring regularly, until tender and all the liquid is absorbed. Add a little more water, if required, during cooking.

HEAT the remaining oil in a frying pan and add the mushrooms and garlic. Fry for 4–5 minutes over a medium heat until starting to brown.

STIR the Philly into the cooked rice. If the mixture is too thick, add a little milk. Remove the rice from the heat and stir in the mushrooms, parsley and black pepper to taste. Serve immediately.

tip Choose your favourite type of mushrooms for this dish – a mixture of chestnut, shiitake and oyster mushrooms works well.

Per serving: energy 377kcal, protein 12.2g, carbohydrate 62.1g, fat 8.9g, equivalent as salt 1.8g

courgette risotto with philly, olives and feta

serves 4 / prep time 5 minutes / cook time 25 minutes

1 tbsp olive oil
1 onion, diced
3 courgettes, sliced
250g risotto rice (Arborio or Carnaroli are best)
1 litre hot vegetable stock
120g Philadelphia Light
20g black olives, pitted and chopped
50g feta

HEAT the oil in a large saucepan, add the onion and courgettes and cook gently for 3–4 minutes, stirring occasionally.

TIP in the rice and stir. Pour in half of the stock, stir well, then continue to stir occasionally until most of it is absorbed. Pour in half the remaining stock and repeat until all the stock is absorbed and the rice is almost cooked. Remove from the heat.

STIR in the Philly and olives, divide among 4 plates and top each with a quarter of the crumbled feta.

Per serving: energy 367kcal, protein 12.0g, carbohydrate 52.9g, fat 11.2g, equivalent as salt 2.3g

philly risotto with butternut squash and sage

serves 4 / prep time 15 minutes / cook time 30 minutes

300g butternut squash, peeled, deseeded and cut into 3cm cubes
1 tbsp olive oil
1.3 litres hot vegetable stock (use a reduced-salt version if you wish)
20g butter
1 small onion, finely chopped
350g risotto rice (Arborio or Carnaroli are best)
100g Philadelphia Light
7 fresh sage leaves, finely shredded
75g peas, cooked
Parmesan shavings, to serve

PREHEAT the oven to 190°C, gas 5. Put half the butternut squash in a roasting tin and drizzle with the oil. Roast for about 20 minutes until tender.

SIMMER the remaining squash in a saucepan with the stock until softened. Tip the squash into a sieve, reserving the stock in a bowl below. Purée the squash using a hand-held blender or liquidiser and set aside. Keep the stock hot.

MELT the butter in a large saucepan and sweat the onion for about 5 minutes, stirring occasionally to stop it catching. Tip in the rice, stir well and add a ladleful of the hot stock while the pan is on the heat. Stir continuously until absorbed. Continue adding the stock, a ladleful at a time, gently stirring between each addition – this gives the risotto its characteristic creamy consistency.

ONCE all the stock has been absorbed, remove from the heat, stir in the puréed squash followed by the Philly, roasted squash, sage and peas. Warm through. Finish with Parmesan shavings.

tip For a more meaty dish, add 1 tablespoon cooked pancetta or bacon pieces just before serving.

Per serving: energy 479kcal, protein 12.0g, carbohydrate 80.0g, fat 12.5g, equivalent as salt 2.8g

smoked salmon, chive, philly and lemon risotto

serves 4 / prep time 5 minutes / cook time 25 minutes

1 tbsp olive oil
1 onion, finely diced
1 garlic clove, crushed
350g risotto rice
1.5 litres hot vegetable stock
120g Philadelphia Chives
170g smoked salmon, cut into pieces
1 lemon
handful of rocket, to serve (optional)

HEAT the oil in a large saucepan and gently cook the onion until soft but not browned. Add the garlic and cook for another 2 minutes, then add the rice and stir to coat in the oil. Add half the stock and stir. Continue to stir occasionally as the stock is absorbed. Add half the remaining stock and repeat until all the stock is absorbed and the rice is tender.

REMOVE from the heat, stir in the Philly and the salmon then grate in the zest of half the lemon and add a squeeze of juice. Serve with a scattering of rocket leaves, if you wish.

tip To reduce the salt content of this dish, use a low-salt stock.

Per serving: energy 462kcal, protein 20.5g, carbohydrate 73.5g, fat 9.7g, equivalent as salt 4.0g

herb risotto

serves 6 / prep time 30 minutes / cook time 30 minutes

20g butter
2 onions, peeled and finely chopped
2 carrots, peeled and finely chopped
320g risotto rice
1.3 litres hot vegetable stock
150g Philadelphia Light
2 tbsp chopped fresh flatleaf parsley
4 tsp chopped fresh dill
6 fresh sage leaves, finely shredded

MELT the butter in a large saucepan. Add the onions and carrots and sweat for about 5 minutes, stirring regularly to avoid burning.

STIR in the rice and coat in the buttery mixture. Add a ladleful of the hot stock and stir continuously until absorbed. Keep adding the stock a ladle at a time and stir gently to release the starch and give the risotto a creamy consistency.

ONCE all the stock has been absorbed by the rice, remove from the heat and stir in the Philly and herbs. Season to taste and, if liked, serve garnished with fresh herbs.

Per serving: energy 290kcal, protein 7.7g, carbohydrate 47.5g, fat 7.2g, equivalent as salt 1.5g

smoked haddock and leek risotto

serves 4 / prep time 10 minutes / cook time 30 minutes

400g undyed smoked haddock
1 tsp olive oil
2 leeks, thinly sliced
300g risotto rice
1.5 litres hot vegetable stock (use
    reduced-salt if you wish)
120g Philadelphia Chives
small bunch of fresh chives, chopped

PUT the haddock in a heatproof dish and pour over boiling water until submerged. Cover with cling film and set aside for 10 minutes to poach. After 10 minutes of poaching, drain the haddock and flake it into chunks.

MEANWHILE heat the oil in a large saucepan, add the leeks and cook gently for 5 minutes until they are softening but not brown. Tip in the rice and stir briefly, then pour in half the stock and stir. Continue to stir regularly until the stock is absorbed then pour in half of the remaining stock. Continue this process until all of the stock has been added.

REMOVE from the heat, add the Philly to the risotto and stir through thoroughly. Add the haddock and chives and stir through gently, taking care not to mash the fish.

Per serving: energy 426kcal, protein 28.6g, carbohydrate 62.8g, fat 6.7g, equivalent as salt 4.5g

asparagus and smoked ham risotto

serves 4 / prep time 5–10 minutes / cook time 30–35 minutes

1 tbsp olive oil
1 red onion, chopped
150g cooked smoked ham, cubed
300g risotto rice
100g asparagus, cut into
   2–3cm pieces
750ml hot vegetable stock
100g Philadelphia Light
fresh flatleaf parsley, to garnish

HEAT the oil in a large saucepan, fry the onion and ham for 2–3 minutes until the onion has softened and begun to brown. Add the rice and asparagus and cook for 1 minute, stirring all the time.

ADD the hot stock, a ladleful at a time, over a moderate heat, stirring well after each addition, allowing the liquid to be absorbed by the rice before adding more. Continue until all the liquid is used up and the rice is cooked through (if the rice is not quite cooked it may be necessary to add more liquid, or if there is too much liquid, let it bubble off).

REMOVE from the heat, add the Philly and stir well to produce a creamy risotto. Serve immediately, garnished with parsley leaves.

tip This dish is also lovely with Parma ham or crispy bacon instead of the cooked ham.

Per serving: energy 392kcal, protein 15.7g, carbohydrate 64.0g, fat 8.1g, equivalent as salt 2.7g

garlicky butternut squash with pumpkin seeds / philly with vegetable parcels / aubergine and courgette layer / creamed almond cauliflower gratin / butternut, cauliflower and chickpea curry / leek, pea and potato rosti / philly dauphinoise / broccoli gratin / leek and garlic gratin / garlic and herb mash / tuscan stuffed red peppers / potatoes and onions in cream sauce / spiced creamed parsnips / roasted vegetable couscous / phillyslaw

VEGETABLES

philly with vegetable pancakes

serves 4 / prep time 10 minutes / cook time 15 minutes

350g mixed vegetables (e.g. baby corn, baby carrots, mangetout, French beans)
150g Philadelphia Chives
3 tbsp milk
8 ready-made pancakes
salad, to serve

CUT the vegetables into even bite-sized pieces and microwave or steam them for 5–8 minutes until tender.

HEAT the Philly with the milk – but do not let it boil. Combine this with the cooked vegetables and a little black pepper.

WARM the pancakes according to the packet instructions and then fill each one with the vegetable mixture. Serve immediately with a little salad.

tip For a non-vegetarian alternative, add 75g cooked chicken to the Philly mixture when warming it through.

Per serving: energy 455kcal, protein 13.4g, carbohydrate 61.5g, fat 18.8g, equivalent as salt 1.5g

aubergine and courgette layer

serves 4 / prep time 20 minutes / cook time 15–20 minutes

1 aubergine
2 courgettes
a little light olive oil
500g carton tomato passata
100g Philadelphia Extra Light
1 egg, beaten
25g finely grated Parmesan

PREHEAT the oven to 220°C, gas 7. Slice the aubergine into ½cm-thick rings and the courgettes into ½cm-thick strips, lay on greased baking sheets, brush lightly with oil and cook in the oven for 10 minutes.

WARM the passata in a small saucepan, but do not boil. Mix together the Philly, egg, three-quarters of the Parmesan and some black pepper in a bowl.

LOWER the oven temperature to 200°C, gas 6 and layer the vegetables in a 1.1-litre ovenproof dish with the passata. Top with the Philly mixture and the remaining Parmesan. Bake for 15–20 minutes until golden brown.

Per serving: energy 166kcal, protein 11.2g, carbohydrate 11.2g, fat 8.0g, equivalent as salt 0.8g

creamed almond cauliflower gratin

serves 6 / prep time 15 minutes / cook time 15 minutes

500g cauliflower florets
100g Philadelphia Garlic & Herbs
25g ground almonds
2 tbsp fresh, flatleaf parsley,
    chopped
10g butter, melted
50g wholemeal breadcrumbs
25g Parmesan, grated

PUT the cauliflower florets in a large saucepan of boiling salted water and cook for 7–9 minutes or until just tender. Drain well.

PLACE the cauliflower in a food processor with the Philly. Process until roughly chopped but not smooth. Stir in the almonds and 1 tablespoon of the parsley. Season to taste. Spoon into an ovenproof serving dish and keep warm.

PREHEAT the grill to High. Mix together the butter, breadcrumbs, Parmesan and remaining parsley. Sprinkle this mixture over the creamed cauliflower and heat under the grill until the topping is golden.

tip The cauliflower may need to be processed in 2 batches, depending on the size of your food processor.

Per serving: energy 143kcal, protein 7.6g, carbohydrate 9.9g, fat 8.4g, equivalent as salt 0.5g

butternut, cauliflower and chickpea curry

serves 4 / prep time 15 minutes / cook time 25 minutes

1 tbsp olive oil
1 onion, peeled and cut into thin
    wedges
1 tbsp korma curry paste
1kg butternut squash, peeled,
    deseeded and cut into
    2–3cm cubes
¼ medium cauliflower, cut into florets
2 large Desiree potatoes, peeled and
    cut into 2–3cm cubes
410g can chopped tomatoes
225g can chickpeas, drained
    and rinsed
375ml vegetable stock
2 tbsp desiccated coconut
125g Philadelphia Light, softened
25g fresh coriander, roughly
    chopped
1–2 tsp lemon juice
steamed rice, to serve

HEAT the oil in a large saucepan. Add the onion and cook gently for 5 minutes or until it is soft and lightly browned. Add the curry paste, stir well and cook for another minute, or until fragrant.

ADD the vegetables, chickpeas, stock and coconut. Bring the mixture to the boil then simmer, covered, over a low heat for about 15 minutes or until the vegetables are just tender. Remove from the heat.

STIR through the Philly until blended. Add the coriander and lemon juice to taste. Serve immediately with steamed rice.

tip Substitute the butternut squash for pumpkin when it is in season.

Per serving: energy 626kcal, protein 19.6g, carbohydrate 83.1g, fat 26.1g, equivalent as salt 2.3g

leek, pea and potato rosti

serves 10 / prep time 25 minutes, plus 30 minutes chilling / cook time 4–5 minutes

4 medium-sized waxy potatoes
1 medium leek, trimmed and
    finely sliced
50g peas, cooked
120g Philadelphia Chives
1 egg
1 tbsp olive oil
1 tbsp plain flour
chopped fresh chives, to garnish
    (optional)

BOIL the unpeeled potatoes in a large saucepan of lightly salted water for 10 minutes. Drain and cool a little then peel away the skins. Coarsely grate the potatoes into strips. Add the leek and peas.

MIX together the Philly and egg in a bowl and season well. Pour over the vegetables and mix lightly together, trying not to break up the grated potato.

TAKE tablespoons of the mixture and mould into cakes, pressing firmly together. Chill for 30 minutes.

HEAT the oil in a non-stick frying pan. Dip each rosti in the flour to lightly dust it then fry for 4–5 minutes each side until golden and cooked. If liked, serve garnished with a few chopped chives.

tip Try adding some chopped cooked bacon to the rosti for a great midweek supper dish.

Per serving: energy 108kcal, protein 4.1g, carbohydrate 15.9g, fat 3.5g, equivalent as salt 0.3g

philly dauphinoise

serves 6 / prep time 20 minutes / cook time 1½ hours

3 medium potatoes, peeled and
   very thinly sliced
10g butter, plus extra for greasing
1 onion, thinly sliced
2 garlic cloves, crushed
150g Philadelphia
200ml milk
25g Gruyère (or low-fat Cheddar),
   finely grated

PREHEAT the oven to 200°C, gas 6 and lightly grease a 16 x 20cm baking dish.

HEAT the butter in a medium saucepan and stir in the onion and garlic. Cook over a low heat until starting to soften then add the Philly and gradually stir in the milk. Continue to cook until the Philly is just melted.

LAYER half the potatoes into the greased dish and pour over half the Philly sauce. Top with the other half of the potatoes and the remaining Philly sauce, seasoning each layer with black pepper.

SPRINKLE with the cheese and bake for 1–1½ hours until golden and the potatoes are cooked through (check with a knife). You will need to cover the dish with foil after 30 minutes of cooking to prevent it browning too much.

tip Use Maris Peer or Charlotte potatoes for the best results, as they keep their shape.

Per serving: energy 192kcal, protein 6.3g, carbohydrate 21.7g, fat 9.6g, equivalent as salt 0.5g

broccoli gratin

serves 4 / prep time 5 minutes / cook time 10–12 minutes

300g broccoli, cut into florets
60g Philadelphia Light
1 tbsp pesto
25g wholemeal breadcrumbs
25g Cheddar, grated

COOK the broccoli in a large saucepan of boiling water for 4–5 minutes or until tender. Drain well and tip into an ovenproof dish.

MIX the Philly with the pesto in a bowl and spoon over the broccoli.

PREHEAT the grill to Medium. Top the Philly mixture with the breadcrumbs and cheese and grill for 5 minutes or until browned.

tip Leeks, cauliflower or fennel work really well as an alternative to broccoli.

Per serving: energy 121kcal, protein 8.1g, carbohydrate 4.8g, fat 7.9g, equivalent as salt 0.5g

leek and garlic gratin

serves 8 / prep time 20–25 minutes / cook time 20 minutes

2 tsp olive oil, plus extra for greasing
1 small onion, thinly chopped
450g leeks, washed and thinly sliced
2 garlic cloves, crushed
180g Philadelphia Light, softened
200ml milk
2 tsp wholegrain mustard
450g waxy potatoes, peeled and
    just cooked
75g Cheddar, grated

PREHEAT the oven to 200°C, gas 6. Lightly grease a 1-litre ovenproof dish.

HEAT the oil in a large saucepan and gently fry the onion, leeks and garlic until soft. Add the Philly, milk and mustard to the leek mixture and season with black pepper. Gently heat, stirring occasionally until the Philly has melted.

SLICE the potatoes thinly and arrange half over the base of the ovenproof dish. Top the potatoes with half the leek mixture and repeat with the remaining potato slices and leek mixture.

SPRINKLE with the grated Cheddar and bake for about 20 minutes or until the top is golden.

tip Waxy potatoes (e.g. Maris Peer or Charlotte) are best for this recipe as they are firm and hold their shape well.

Per serving: energy 165kcal, protein 7.9g, carbohydrate 15.1g, fat 8.5g, equivalent as salt 0.6g

garlic and herb mash

serves 4 / prep time 10 minutes / cook time 15–20 minutes

450g floury potatoes, peeled
100g Philadelphia Garlic & Herbs,
    softened
a dash of milk (optional)
mixed fresh herbs, to garnish

CUT the potatoes into 3cm chunks and place them in a large saucepan of water. Bring to the boil and cook for 15–20 minutes or until tender. Drain and mash the potatoes together with the Philly and add a little milk if you like a softer consistency. Serve warm, garnished with a few fresh herbs.

tip Floury potatoes (e.g. Desiree or King Edward) are best used for mashing as they are softer and have a dry texture, which makes lovely fluffy mash.

Per serving: energy 120kcal, protein 4.1g, carbohydrate 20.1g, fat 3.0g, equivalent as salt 0.3g

tuscan stuffed red peppers

serves 8 / prep time 20 minutes / cook time 20 minutes

4 red peppers
1 tbsp olive oil
175g mixed long grain and wild rice
4 tomatoes, skinned, quartered
   and deseeded
4 spring onions, finely chopped
40g black olives, pitted and sliced
2 tbsp white wine vinegar
2 garlic cloves, peeled and sliced
150g Philadelphia Basil

PREHEAT the oven to 220°C, gas 7. Cut the peppers in half lengthways through the stalk and remove the core and seeds. Arrange on a baking sheet, cut-side uppermost, and brush with a little of the oil. Bake for about 15 minutes or until tender. Leave to cool.

MEANWHILE, cook the rice following the packet instructions. Drain and rinse well with cold water.

ROUGHLY chop the tomatoes and mix into the rice with the spring onions and olives.

WHISK together the remaining olive oil, vinegar, garlic and Philly and season well. Pour this dressing over the rice and mix together. Pile the rice into the pepper halves and arrange on a serving plate.

tip This filling mixture is delicious served as a rice salad.

You could substitute Philadelphia Chives for Philadelphia Basil, if you prefer.

Per serving: energy 164kcal, protein 4.4g, carbohydrate 26.3g, fat 5.2g, equivalent as salt 0.5g

potatoes and onions in cream sauce

serves 4 / prep time 20 minutes / cook time 16–17 minutes

700g medium potatoes, peeled and
   cut into even-sized large pieces
300g shallots, peeled
200ml hot chicken stock
120g Philadelphia Light

COOK the potatoes in a large saucepan of boiling water for 10–12 minutes until tender when tested with a knife. Drain.

PLACE the shallots in a pan, add the stock and simmer with the lid on for 15 minutes until tender. Stir in the Philly and add the cooked potatoes to the sauce. Heat gently for 1–2 minutes, adjust the seasonings to taste and serve.

tip If the shallots are quite large, simply cut them in half before cooking.

Per serving: energy 195kcal, protein 7.4g, carbohydrate 33.9g, fat 4.1g, equivalent as salt 1.0g

spiced creamed parsnips

serves 4 / prep time 10 minutes / cook time 20 minutes

15g butter
450g parsnips, peeled and diced,
    any woody bits discarded
100g Philadelphia Chives
freshly grated nutmeg

PUT the butter in a saucepan and heat until it begins to foam and brown. Add the parsnips and stir before adding 100ml water.

COVER the pan and bring to the boil. Reduce the heat to a gentle simmer and cook for about 20 minutes, stirring occasionally, or until the parsnips are completely tender. If all the cooking liquid evaporates during the cooking, add a little more.

PLACE the parsnips and any residual liquid into a food processor. Add the Philly and some nutmeg. Process to a purée. Season to taste and serve hot, sprinkled with more nutmeg.

tip If liked, substitute 100g of the parsnips for 100g peeled, diced apple to give a fruity note to this vegetable dish.

Per serving: energy 140kcal, protein 4.2g, carbohydrate 15.1g, fat 7.6g, equivalent as salt 0.5g

roasted vegetable couscous

serves 4 / prep time 20 minutes / cook time 30 minutes

1 aubergine
1 yellow pepper, cored and
    deseeded
1 red onion, peeled
1 tbsp olive oil
200g couscous
2 tbsp skimmed milk
75g Philadelphia Extra Light,
    softened
a few fresh mint leaves
zest and juice of 1 lemon

PREHEAT the oven to 220°C, gas 7. Cut the vegetables into 2–3cm chunks, toss in the oil and place in a roasting tin. Cook for 25–30 minutes or until starting to turn golden around the edges.

MAKE the couscous following the packet instructions.

IN a small bowl, stir the milk into the Philly a little at a time. Add the mint, lemon juice and zest. Leave to stand while you stir the vegetables into the couscous, then drizzle with the Philly dressing to serve.

tip This can be made in advance and served cold. Pour the dressing over just before serving.

Per serving: energy 280kcal, protein 10.8g, carbohydrate 46.7g, fat 6.0g, equivalent as salt 2.0g

phillyslaw

serves 8 / prep time 15 minutes

1 celeriac, approx. 450g peeled
    weight
450g carrots, peeled
180g Philadelphia Extra Light
juice of 1 lemon
25g walnuts, roughly chopped

USING a food processor, finely grate the celeriac and carrots and place in a large bowl (alternatively, do this with a hand-held grater).

COMBINE the Philly, lemon juice and black pepper, add to the grated vegetables and mix well together. Serve scattered with the walnuts.

tip This is a much lighter coleslaw using celeriac. If you cannot find it, use finely sliced celery instead. It will keep covered in the fridge for 2–3 days. Ideal for parties.

Per serving: energy 76kcal, protein 4.2g, carbohydrate 7.0g, fat 3.6g, equivalent as salt 0.5g

maple and pecan philly ice cream / lemon grove gelato / vanilla marsala mousse / lemon crêpes / 5-minute fruit brûlée / creamy chocolate and orange cups / brandied chocolate cherry dessert / philly ginger puds / tiramisù / grilled peaches with marsala cream / summer berry charlotte / elderflower philly pannacotta with poached plums / frosty apricot ice cream / baked pear and vanilla cheesecake / baked chocolate and orange cheesecake / baked lemon and sultana cheesecake / apricot crumble cheesecake / fruity frozen cheesecake / cool and creamy cheesecake / marbled warm chocolate fudge cake / sticky toffee squares / carrot cake / cheesecake brownies

SWEET TREATS

maple and pecan philly ice cream

serves 8 / prep time 20 minutes, plus overnight freezing

250g Philadelphia
200ml condensed milk
200ml soured cream
3 tbsp maple syrup
30g pecan nuts, chopped

MIX together the Philly, condensed milk and soured cream. Stir in the maple syrup. Spoon into a freezerproof container and freeze for 3–4 hours or until semi-frozen.

REMOVE the ice cream from the freezer, decant into a mixing bowl and whisk to break up the ice crystals. Stir in the pecan pieces and spoon back into the freezerproof container. Freeze until completely frozen, preferably overnight.

REMOVE from the freezer 20–30 minutes before serving to soften slightly.

tip Alternatively, place the mixture in an ice-cream maker until frozen.

Per serving: energy 277kcal, protein 5.5g, carbohydrate 20.1g, fat 19.9g, equivalent as salt 0.3g

lemon grove gelato

serves 8 / prep time 25 minutes, plus overnight freezing / cook time 15 minutes

200g Philadelphia
300ml condensed milk
150ml Greek yoghurt
grated zest of 1 lemon and
    2 tbsp juice
2 tbsp lemon or orange curd,
    softened

MIX together the Philly, condensed milk and yoghurt. Stir in the lemon zest and juice.

SPOON into a freezerproof container and place in the freezer for 3–4 hours or until semi-frozen.

REMOVE the ice cream from the freezer and decant into a mixing bowl. Whisk to break up the ice crystals, spoon back into the freezerproof container then carefully swirl in the lemon or orange curd to give a rippled effect. Freeze until completely frozen, preferably overnight.

REMOVE from the freezer around 30 minutes before serving to soften slightly. Serve in scoops and decorate as you wish.

Per serving: energy 241kcal, protein 6.2g, carbohydrate 24.6g, fat 13.8g, equivalent as salt 0.3g

vanilla marsala mousse

200ml milk
1 vanilla pod
2 egg yolks
60g caster sugar
200g Philadelphia Light
11g sachet powdered gelatine
150ml double cream,
    lightly whipped
75ml Marsala

POUR the milk into a small saucepan, then cut the vanilla pod in half lengthways, scrape out the seeds into the milk and drop in the pod. Bring to the boil, simmer gently for 5 minutes then leave to infuse and cool for 30 minutes. Remove the vanilla pod.

WHISK together the egg yolks and sugar until thick and creamy. Mix in the vanilla milk and return to the saucepan. Heat gently, stirring continuously, to thicken the custard, but do not let it boil. Remove from the heat and stir in the Philly until melted.

COVER the surface of the custard with cling film and allow to cool for about 30 minutes. When cool, put 3 tablespoons warm water into a small heatproof bowl and sprinkle over the gelatine. Stand the bowl over a pan of simmering water and heat until dissolved.

FOLD the whipped cream and Marsala into the cool custard then quickly stir in the dissolved gelatine. Divide the mixture between 6 dessert glasses and chill for about 3 hours or until set.

tip This dessert is particularly delicious accompanied by poached spiced plums or nectarines.

Per serving: energy 277kcal, protein 6.8g, carbohydrate 15.4g, fat 19.7g, equivalent as salt 0.5g

lemon crêpes

serves 10 / prep time 20 minutes, plus 30 minutes chilling / cook time 30 minutes

125g plain flour
3 eggs, lightly beaten
250ml milk
200g Philadelphia Light, softened
125g cottage cheese
100g sultanas
2 tbsp caster sugar
grated zest of 1 lemon
20g butter
icing sugar, to dust

SIFT the flour into a bowl. Make a well in the centre and gradually whisk in the beaten eggs and milk until smooth. Refrigerate this batter for 30 minutes.

COMBINE the Philly, cottage cheese, sultanas, sugar and lemon zest until smooth.

MELT a little of the butter in a small non-stick frying pan, and when it is hot, pour a little of the batter evenly into the pan. Cook the crêpe until lightly browned underneath, then turn it over and cook the other side until golden. Set aside and repeat to make a total of 10 crêpes, layering them between greaseproof paper.

SPOON 2 tablespoons of the Philly mixture into the centre of each crêpe. Fold in the sides to make a parcel and dust with a little icing sugar to serve.

tips Serve these with a warm filling by arranging the parcels in an ovenproof dish. Heat through in an oven set to 150°C, gas 2 for 5 minutes before dusting with icing sugar.

Alternatively, serve with a lemon sauce: combine 2 tablespoons butter, a little lemon juice and 2 tablespoons sugar in a pan and simmer for 2 minutes. Drizzle over the warm parcels and serve.

Per serving: energy 179kcal, protein 7.4g, carbohydrate 23.3g, fat 6.8g, equivalent as salt 0.4g

5-minute fruit brûlée

serves 6 / prep time 10 minutes / cook time 5 minute

200g Philadelphia Light
150g 0% fat Greek yoghurt
175g ripe soft fruit (e.g. raspberries,
    strawberries, blackberries,
    blueberries)
6 tbsp fruit compote
6 tbsp demerara sugar

PREHEAT the grill to High. Beat together the Philly and Greek yoghurt until well combined.

CUT any larger berries into small pieces. Mix all the berries with the fruit compote and divide between 6 large ramekin dishes. Spoon over the Philly mixture and smooth with the back of a spoon.

SPOON the sugar evenly over the Philly and place on a baking sheet. Pop under the grill until the sugar is bubbling and has caramelised. Leave for a few minutes to allow the sugar to crisp and cool a little before eating.

tip This can also be made with frozen fruit. Thaw the fruit at room temperature and use as above, draining away any excess juice if necessary.

Per serving: energy 174kcal, protein 4.9g, carbohydrate 31.4g, fat 4.0g, equivalent as salt 0.4g

creamy chocolate and orange cups

serves 8 / prep time 20 minutes, plus 2 hours chilling / cook time 5 minutes

275ml double cream
100g dark chocolate, plus extra
    grated chocolate to decorate
160g Philadelphia Light
30g icing sugar
finely grated zest of ½ orange and
    1 tbsp juice

HEAT the cream in a saucepan until almost boiling. Remove from the heat. Break the chocolate into pieces and stir into the cream until melted.

POUR the mixture into 8 small dessert glasses. Chill for about 2 hours or until set.

MEANWHILE, mix together the Philly, icing sugar, orange juice and zest until smooth. Spoon or pipe a layer of the Philly mixture over each chocolate dessert. Serve immediately, topped with the grated chocolate or chill until ready to serve.

tip This is a rich, indulgent dessert, so serve small portions, perhaps in shot glasses.

Per serving: energy 281kcal, protein 2.9g, carbohydrate 13.4g, fat 24.3g, equivalent as salt 0.3g

brandied chocolate cherry dessert

serves 6 / prep time 15 minutes, plus 1 hour chilling

80g dark chocolate, melted
150g fresh black cherries, halved
    and pitted, or 425g can cherries,
    drained, halved and pitted
3 tbsp brandy
20g caster sugar
200g Philadelphia Light, softened

ALLOW the melted chocolate to cool a little, then stir in the cherries.

IN a separate bowl, stir the brandy and the sugar into the Philly.

SWIRL the 2 mixtures together to give a rippled effect, then divide it between 6 small dessert glasses. Chill for at least 1 hour before serving.

tip Delicious served with some fresh seasonal fruit on the side.

Per serving: energy 166kcal, protein 3.7g, carbohydrate 16.8g, fat 8.3g, equivalent as salt 0.3g

philly ginger puds

serves 6 / prep time 10 minutes, plus 30 minutes chilling

6 x 1–2cm-thick slices Jamaica
    cake or ginger cake (approx.
    150g weight)
3 ginger nuts
200g Philadelphia Light
1 tsp vanilla essence
zest of 2 oranges, chopped into
    segments and pith removed
6 tsp dark muscovado sugar

CUT each cake slice into 6 discs and place 1 at the
bottom of each of 6 medium-sized ramekins.

BASH up the ginger nuts, mix with the Philly, vanilla
essence, orange zest, segments and a little of the juice
saved from the chopping. Fill the ramekins with
the mixture.

SPRINKLE sugar on top and refrigerate until the
sugar goes gooey (about 30 minutes). Decorate with
orange zest and enjoy!

tip If the cake discs do not fit perfectly, use some
of the leftover cake to fill in any gaps.

Per serving: energy 202kcal, protein 4.5g, carbohydrate 30.5g, fat 7.2g, equivalent as salt 0.5g

tiramisù

serves 6 / prep time 15 minutes, plus 3–4 hours or overnight chilling

100ml espresso coffee, chilled
2 tsp Amaretto
200g Philadelphia
100ml natural yoghurt
1 tsp vanilla essence
25g icing sugar
115g sponge fingers
2–3 tsp cocoa powder, sieved

LINE a small loaf tin with cling film. Place the espresso, 50ml water and Amaretto in a shallow bowl and set aside. In a small bowl, beat together the Philly, yoghurt, vanilla and icing sugar until softened.

DIP half the sponge fingers in the coffee mixture and line the base of the loaf tin with them. Spread half of the Philly mixture over the sponges in the tin and then repeat to make a second layer.

COVER and leave in the fridge for 3–4 hours, or preferably overnight. Dust the top with a thick layer of cocoa powder, then carefully lift the tiramisù out of the tin using the cling flim. Carefully slice before serving.

tip This dessert is best left chilling overnight so that the flavours fully develop.

Per serving: energy 201kcal, protein 5.0g, carbohydrate 23.3g, fat 9.7g, equivalent as salt 1.1g

grilled peaches with marsala cream

serves 4 / prep time 10 minutes / cook time 8 minutes

120g Philadelphia Light, softened
1 tbsp caster sugar
2 tsp Marsala or sherry
4 large ripe peaches
2 tbsp light muscovado sugar
20g flaked almonds, toasted

BEAT together the Philly, caster sugar and Marsala or sherry until smooth. Cover and refrigerate.

PREHEAT the grill to High. Cut each peach in half and remove the stones. Sprinkle the cut side with the muscovado sugar. Place the peaches on a baking sheet and pop under the grill for 6–8 minutes or until the peaches have softened and the sugar is bubbling and golden.

ARRANGE the peaches on serving plates, sprinkle with the almonds and serve with a spoonful of Marsala Philly cream. Serve immediately.

tip Alternatively, replace the muscovado sugar with a dusting of icing sugar and pop the peaches onto a hot barbecue until softened and golden.

Per serving: energy 185kcal, protein 5.0g, carbohydrate 28.5g, fat 6.4g, equivalent as salt 0.3g

summer berry charlotte

serves 8 / prep time 20–25 minutes, plus 2–3 hours or overnight chilling

25–30 sponge fingers
290g can mixed berries in syrup, drained and syrup reserved
5g powdered gelatine (about half a sachet)
200g Philadelphia Light, softened
1 tbsp caster sugar
125ml double cream
225g fresh strawberries, halved or quartered
fresh raspberries and raspberry sauce (made from puréed raspberries), to serve

LINE a small loaf tin with cling film. Trim the sponge fingers to line the base and sides of the tin, leaving enough fingers for the top. Reserve about one-third of the syrup. Dip the sponges in the remaining syrup and line the tin with them straight away.

DISSOLVE the gelatine in 100ml warm water in a small heatproof bowl set over a pan of simmering water. Beat the Philly and sugar in a bowl with an electric mixer until smooth. Stir in the cream and the gelatine mixture. Fold in the mixed berries and strawberries. Pour the mixture into the prepared tin. Top with the reserved sponge fingers and brush with the reserved syrup.

CHILL for 2–3 hours or overnight until set. Invert onto a serving plate and serve sliced, with fresh raspberries and raspberry sauce, if desired.

tip Work quickly when you are dipping the sponges into the syrup or they may fall apart. Not all of the sponge fingers have to be dipped as they will absorb liquid from the Philly mixture as it sets.

Per serving: energy 268kcal, protein 5.3g, carbohydrate 34.5g, fat 12.2g, equivalent as salt 1.1g

elderflower philly pannacotta with poached plums

serves 8 / prep time 20 minutes, plus 4 hours chilling / cook time 15 minutes

olive oil, for greasing
11g sachet powdered gelatine
400ml single cream
40g caster sugar
4 tbsp elderflower cordial
200g Philadelphia Light
300g red or yellow plums, quartered
    and stones removed
50g light muscovado sugar
½ tsp ground cinnamon

LIGHTLY oil 8 individual dariole moulds. Put 3 tablespoons very hot water into a small heatproof bowl and sprinkle over the gelatine. Stand the bowl over a saucepan of simmering water and heat gently until dissolved.

PUT the cream and caster sugar in a saucepan and heat gently. Bring the cream almost to boiling point, stirring to ensure the sugar has dissolved. Remove from the heat, stir in the elderflower cordial then whisk in the Philly until melted. Stir in the dissolved gelatine, divide the mixture between the moulds and chill for around 4 hours or until set.

MEANWHILE, put the plums in a pan with 50ml water, the muscovado sugar and cinnamon. Heat gently, stirring occasionally, until the sugar has dissolved, then simmer for 7–9 minutes or until the plums are cooked. Chill well before serving with the pannacotta, turned out of their moulds.

tip Try using fresh rhubarb or gooseberries in place of plums for this recipe.

Per serving: energy 209kcal, protein 5.1g, carbohydrate16.3g, fat 12.5g, equivalent as salt 0.3g

frosty apricot ice cream

serves 8–10 / prep time 15 minutes, plus freezing time

425g can apricots, in fruit juice
150g Philadelphia, softened
500g fresh chilled custard

DRAIN the apricots, reserving the juice. Finely chop the apricots.

PLACE the Philly in a bowl with 2–3 tablespoons of the fruit juice. Beat until soft and creamy, then gradually stir in the apricots and custard.

SPOON into a freezerproof container and freeze for 3–4 hours or until semi-frozen. Remove the ice cream from the freezer, decant into a mixing bowl and whisk to break up the ice crystals, then spoon back into the freezerproof container. Freeze until completely frozen, preferably overnight.

REMOVE from the freezer about 30 minutes before serving, to soften.

tip Alternatively, place in an ice-cream maker until frozen or freeze the ice-cream mixture in a loaf tin, remove 30 minutes before serving and serve in slices.

Per serving: energy 126kcal, protein 3.1g, carbohydrate 15.3g, fat 6.4g, equivalent as salt 0.3g

baked pear and vanilla cheesecake

serves 12 / prep time 25 minutes, plus chilling / cook time 1¼ hours

150g ginger nuts, crushed
50g butter or margarine, melted
600g Philadelphia, softened
225g caster sugar
3 eggs, lightly beaten
1 vanilla pod
200ml single cream
410g can pear halves, well
   drained and sliced

PREHEAT the oven to 150°C, gas 2. Grease and line the base of a 20cm springform cake tin. Combine the biscuit crumbs and butter or margarine and press into the base of the prepared tin. Chill.

BEAT the Philly and sugar until smooth, add the eggs and mix until combined. Split the vanilla pod lengthwise, scrape the seeds out into the cream and gently fold through the Philly mixture. Pour onto the prepared base. Bake for 1¼ hours.

ALLOW the cheesecake to cool completely in the oven. Place the pear slices onto the cheesecake and chill before serving.

tip This can also be made in individual mini cheesecake tins or ovenproof dishes.

Per serving: energy 342kcal, protein 5.9g, carbohydrate 33.3g, fat 21.6g, equivalent as salt 0.7g

baked chocolate and orange cheesecake

serves 12 / prep time 20–25 minutes, plus chilling / cook time 1 hour

150g butter, plus extra for greasing
150g orange-flavoured chocolate
    biscuits, crushed
75g caster sugar
2 eggs, separated
450g Philadelphia Light, softened
1½ tbsp warm water
15g cocoa powder, sifted
1 tbsp custard powder
4 tbsp single cream
finely grated zest and juice of ½
    orange
icing sugar, orange rind and
    chocolate curls, to decorate

PREHEAT the oven to 170°C, gas 3. Grease and line the base of a 22cm springform cake tin. Melt 50g of the butter and stir it into the biscuit crumbs. Press the biscuit mixture into the base of the prepared tin and chill until required.

CREAM together the remaining butter and the sugar until light and fluffy. Gradually beat in the egg yolks then the softened Philly. In a separate bowl, mix the warm water, cocoa and custard powders together to form a firm paste. Slowly add the cream to the paste and then combine with the Philly mixture. Gradually add the orange zest and juice and stir until evenly mixed.

WHISK the egg whites in a bowl until stiff then fold them gently into the Philly mixture. Pour onto the biscuit base and bake for 1 hour. Leave the cheesecake to cool completely in the oven. Decorate the top with a sprinkling of sifted icing sugar, orange rind and chocolate curls.

tip Leaving the cheesecake in the oven to cool completely reduces the risk of it cracking.

Per serving: energy 275kcal, protein 5.5g, carbohydrate 19.7g, fat 19.8g, equivalent as salt 0.8g

baked lemon and sultana cheesecake

serves 10 / prep time 25–30 minutes, plus overnight chilling / cook time 1–1¼ hours

50g self-raising flour
½ tsp baking powder
50g butter, softened, or soft
   margarine
275g caster sugar
5 large eggs
400g Philadelphia, softened
40g plain flour
grated zest and juice of 1 lemon
75g sultanas
142ml carton soured cream

PREHEAT the oven to 170°C, gas 3. Grease and line the base of a 22cm springform cake tin. Sift the self-raising flour and baking powder into a bowl. Add the butter or margarine, 50g of the sugar and 1 egg. Mix well then beat for 2–3 minutes. Spread the mixture over the base of the prepared tin.

SEPARATE the remaining eggs. Whisk together the egg yolks and remaining sugar until thick and creamy. Add to the Philly and mix in well. Fold the plain flour into the Philly mixture along with the lemon zest and juice, sultanas and soured cream.

WHISK the egg whites in a bowl until stiff then fold them into the cheese mixture. Pour this over the mixture in the tin. Bake for 1–1¼hours until firm, yet spongy to the touch. Turn off the oven and leave the cheesecake inside for 1 hour with the door ajar. Remove the cheesecake from the oven and leave to cool completely. Chill in the fridge, preferably overnight, before serving.

tip This cheesecake is best left to chill in the fridge overnight or it can be a little soft and sticky to slice.

Per serving: energy 376kcal, protein 8.0g, carbohydrate 42.9g, fat 20.4g, equivalent as salt 0.7g

apricot crumble cheesecake

serves 12 / prep time 20–25 minutes, plus 2 hours setting

150g sweet oaty biscuits, crushed
60g butter or margarine, melted
50g roasted hazelnuts, finely
    chopped
1 tsp ground cinnamon
½ tsp grated nutmeg
400g Philadelphia, softened
150g caster sugar
11g sachet powdered gelatine
2 tbsp lemon juice
250ml double cream, lightly whipped
425g can apricot halves in fruit juice,
    drained and halved

GREASE and line the base of a 20cm springform cake tin. Combine the biscuit crumbs, butter, hazelnuts and spices. Divide this mixture in half (saving the other half) and press into the base of the prepared tin. Chill until firm.

BEAT together the Philly and sugar until smooth.

DISSOLVE the gelatine in 3 tablespoons (or 75ml) of warm water in a bowl set over a saucepan of simmering water. Beat the gelatine and lemon juice into the Philly mixture until well blended. Fold in the whipped cream and apricots. Pour the mixture over the biscuit crumbs in the tin.

TOP the cheesecake with the remaining crumb mixture. Chill for 2 hours or until set. Serve straight from the fridge.

tip For a variation on the classic biscuit base, mix a tablespoon of desiccated coconut into the biscuit crumbs.

Per serving: energy 369kcal, protein 4.8g, carbohydrate 24.7g, fat 28.7g, equivalent as salt 0.5g

fruity frozen cheesecake

serves 10 / prep time 20 minutes, plus 2–3 hours freezing

150g low-fat digestive biscuits, crushed
50g butter or margarine, melted
200g Philadelphia, softened
200g caster sugar
250ml raspberry juice
150g fresh or frozen raspberries
200ml whipping cream, lightly whipped

LINE the base of a 20cm springform cake tin. Combine the biscuit crumbs and melted butter or margarine and press into the base of the prepared tin. Chill.

BEAT the Philly and sugar together until smooth. Gently stir in the raspberry juice, raspberries and whipped cream. Spoon into the prepared base.

FREEZE for 2–3 hours or until firm. Remove from the freezer about 15 minutes before serving to allow it to soften slightly.

tip If you can't find raspberry juice, use raspberry and cranberry or a raspberry and apple mix. Darker-coloured juices may alter the colour of the cheesecake mixture, giving a lovely pale pink hue.

Per serving: energy 328kcal, protein 2.9g, carbohydrate 36.7g, fat 19.4g, equivalent as salt 0.5g

cool and creamy cheesecake

serves 10 / prep time 30 minutes, plus 3–4 hours setting

75g butter or margarine
200g digestive biscuits, crushed
450g Philadelphia Light, softened
100ml milk
150g caster sugar
zest and juice of 1 lemon
11g sachet of powdered gelatine
100ml double cream, lightly whipped
fresh fruits(e.g. figs, nectarines,
    blackberries and redcurrants),
    to decorate

LINE the base of a 20cm springform cake tin. Melt the butter or margarine and mix with the crushed biscuit crumbs. Press into the base of the prepared tin and chill.

BEAT the Philly until soft and smooth. Add the milk, sugar, lemon zest and juice and mix thoroughly.

DISSOLVE the gelatine in 3 tablespoons of warm water in a small heatproof bowl set over a pan of simmering water. Add to the Philly mixture then fold in the cream. Pour onto the crumb base and chill in the fridge for 3–4 hours until set.

JUST before serving, remove the cheesecake from the tin and decorate with fresh fruit.

tip For an extra-fruity version, replace the lemon juice and milk with 250g mashed or puréed soft fruit (e.g. raspberries or strawberries) and add to the Philly with the sugar.

Per serving: energy 353kcal, protein 6.5g, carbohydrate 31.8g, fat 23.1g, equivalent as salt 0.8g

marbled warm chocolate fudge cake

serves 12 / prep time 25 minutes / cook time 45 minutes

140g butter, plus extra for greasing
120g plain chocolate
170g caster sugar
100ml very hot water
140g self-raising flour
40g cocoa powder
2 eggs
150g Philadelphia Light

PREHEAT the oven to 180°C, gas 4 and grease and line a 23cm loose-bottomed cake tin.

MELT the butter and chocolate in a heatproof bowl set over a saucepan of simmering water. Remove from the heat and stir in 140g of the caster sugar and the hot water, then the flour and cocoa. Beat in the eggs one at a time. Mix the Philly with the remaining caster sugar.

POUR the chocolate mixture into the prepared tin. Spoon the sweetened Philly randomly over the surface of the chocolate mixture and swirl with the tip of a knife.

BAKE for about 45 minutes or until risen and springy to the touch. Leave to cool for 10 minutes before removing from the tin.

tip This is a rich, moist cake best served warm and in small portions. If liked, add the finely grated rind of half an orange to the sweetened Philly.

Per serving: energy 287kcal, protein 4.5g, carbohydrate 33.6g, fat 15.8g, equivalent as salt 0.5g

sticky toffee squares

serves 16 / prep time 25 minutes / cook time 40 minutes

150g stoned dates, roughly chopped
50g sultanas
1 tsp bicarbonate of soda
150g butter
150g caster sugar
2 eggs
175g self-raising flour
180g Philadelphia
4 tsp dulce de leche
25g walnuts, chopped

PREHEAT the oven to 180°C, gas 4 and grease and line a 22 x 18cm baking tin.

PUT the dates and sultanas in a saucepan with 250ml water and bring to the boil. Simmer for 5 minutes to soften. Remove from the heat and stir in the bicarbonate of soda. Leave to cool a little.

CREAM together the butter and sugar until light and fluffy. Gradually add the eggs, beating well after each addition.

GENTLY fold in the flour then stir in the date mixture, including any liquid. Spoon into the prepared tin and bake for 35–40 minutes until well risen and firm to the touch. Leave to cool completely before removing from the tin.

TO make the toffee frosting, beat together the Philly and dulce de leche – the mixture will thicken as you whisk it. Swirl over the cake and sprinkle with walnuts. Cut into squares.

tip Eat the same day or keep refrigerated overnight in an airtight container.

Per serving : energy 234kcal, protein 3.4g, carbohydrate 28.3g, fat 12.6g, equivalent as salt 0.5g

carrot cake

serves 10 / prep time 20–25 minutes / cook time 45–50 minutes

2 eggs, separated
225g light muscovado sugar
175g butter or margarine, melted
150g wholemeal flour
1 tsp baking powder
½ tsp mixed spice
25g chopped walnuts
25g sultanas
175g carrots, finely grated

For the topping:
200g Philadelphia
50g icing sugar, sifted
finely grated zest of ½ lemon

PREHEAT the oven to 190°C, gas 5. Grease and line the base of a 20cm springform cake tin.

CREAM together the egg yolks, sugar and melted butter or margarine. Stir in 2 tablespoons warm water. Place the remaining cake ingredients in a bowl, make a well in the centre, add the egg mixture and beat thoroughly.

WHISK the egg whites in a bowl until standing in soft peaks. Fold carefully into the cake mixture. Spoon the mixture into the prepared tin and bake for 45–50 minutes or until a skewer inserted in the centre comes out clean. Allow to cool slightly, then turn out and cool completely on a wire rack.

CREAM together the Philly and icing sugar until soft and creamy. Stir in most of the lemon zest and spread over the cake. Decorate with a little more grated lemon zest if desired.

Per serving: energy 374kcal, protein 5.0g, carbohydrate 41.7g, fat 22.4g, equivalent as salt 0.7g

cheesecake brownies

serves 12 / prep time 10 minutes / cook time 35–40 minutes

125g butter
125g dark chocolate, chopped
200g dark muscovado sugar
3 eggs, lightly beaten
50g plain flour, sifted
50g cocoa powder
¼ tsp baking powder
200g Philadelphia Light
50g caster sugar

PREHEAT the oven to 180˚C, gas 4. Grease and line an 18 x 28cm rectangular cake tin. Combine the butter, chocolate and muscovado sugar in a medium saucepan. Stir over a medium heat until the chocolate and butter have melted. Remove from the heat, allow to cool slightly and whisk in the eggs.

ADD the flour, cocoa and baking powder and stir until well combined. Pour into the prepared tin.

BEAT the Philly and caster sugar until smooth and creamy. Spoon randomly over the chocolate mixture and swirl with the tip of a knife. Bake for 35–40 minutes or until cooked through. Allow to cool before slicing.

tip Perfect served with afternoon tea or with coffee at the end of a meal. If you're feeling really decadent and you don't mind raising the calorie level of this recipe, allow yourself a chocolate truffle too!

Per serving: energy 282kcal, protein 4.9g, carbohydrate 32.4g, fat 15.9g, equivalent as salt 0.5g

index

acknowledgements

The Philadelphia team would like to thank everyone who has helped create this book.

Recipe Development and Testing Team
Emma Warner, Hazel Middleton, Wendy Strang, Alison Clarkson

Photography
Dan Jones, Will Heap and Adrian Lander, Photographers

Sonja Edridge, Sal Henley, Linda Brushfield and Sarah Tildesley, Food Stylists

Morag Farquhra and Rachel Jukes, Prop Stylists

Marketing Team
Jennie Atkinson and Rebecca Pilling
Victoria Milner and Carly Jackson

Thanks also go to:
The team at Ebury Press for their support and guidance, and the Law, Regulatory and Corporate Affairs teams for their enthusiasm and commitment throughout the project.